LOADED!

BECOME
A MILLIONAIRE
OVERNIGHT AND
LOSE 20 POUNDS
IN 2 WEEKS,
OR YOUR
MONEY BACK!*

WILLIE GEIST and BOYD McDONNELL

*with **The Dollar Bills***

*Good luck trying to get your money back.

St. Martin's Griffin New York

To the Winklevoss Twins,
for your warmth and guidance

LOADED! Copyright © 2011 by Willie Geist and Boyd McDonnell. All rights reserved. Printed in the United States of America. For information, address St. Martin's Press, 175 Fifth Avenue, New York, N.Y. 10010.

www.stmartins.com

Library of Congress Cataloging-in-Publication Data

Geist, Willie.
    Loaded! : become a millionaire overnight and lose 20 pounds in 2 weeks, or your money back *good luck trying to get your money back / Willie Geist and Boyd McDonnell with the Dollar Bills. — 1st ed.
        p. cm.
    ISBN 978-0-312-64153-5
    1. Finance, Personal—Humor.   2. Money—Humor.
I. McDonnell, Boyd.   II. Title.
    PN6231.F47G45 2011
    818'.602—dc22

2011002710

First Edition: May 2011

10 9 8 7 6 5 4 3 2 1

Also by Willie Geist

*American Freak Show: The Completely Fabricated Stories
of Our New National Treasures*

Introduction

By Willie Geist and Boyd McDonnell

It's a dream as old as America itself: giving your children a better life than your own. It's not a dream we necessarily share (most of our dreams involve Bruce Willis and underground mixed martial arts), but it's just kind of embarrassing if your kids end up being losers. Today, that American promise to leave the world better than we found it is, for the first time, in jeopardy. The humbling decline of the United States economy has made it very likely that our kids will, in fact, be losers.

For more than a decade we've been close friends and

collaborators (a euphemism for "two guys who take frequent cruises together without their families"). We both have young children and we work hard to provide for them—to give them that better life. Truth be told, we work hard mostly to make money for ourselves so we can buy ski boats and $70 filets, but the children thing sounds more noble.

Growing up in the American suburbs, we each faced hardships that remain difficult to talk about to this day. You've heard the romanticized clichés about growing up in the ghetto and making it out (see Jay-Z, 50 Cent). We may not have had gunfire in our neighborhoods, but that doesn't mean we didn't sometimes have our feelings hurt.

As a high school junior in St. Louis, Boyd was forced to drive a stick shift minivan, without a cassette player, for an entire year. The other kids at school would cruise the parking lot in their Jeeps and expensive convertibles, blasting music from their sweet, removable-faceplate stereos. Boyd was ashamed, stuck grinding the minivan into second gear to the static-laced sounds of whatever the AM radio could pick up. To this day, the smell of a burning clutch makes him clammy. He swore every time that minivan jerked out of the school parking lot: Never again.

Willie, meanwhile, mowed lawns in suburban New Jersey with a manual push mower for two straight summers just to make enough money to buy the *Major League* trilogy on VHS. It wasn't until the end of that second summer that he realized Kevin Costner wasn't in *Major League*. Tragically, Willie had been thinking of *Bull Durham* the whole time (or maybe it was *Field of Dreams*). As he emptied yet another bag full of his neighbors' grass clippings, he swore up and down: Never again.

Why do we dredge up these painful experiences? Because they left deep scars (kind of like when 50 Cent was shot nine times—the event shaped him and left deep scars). More importantly, the trauma of these events created the shared desire to protect our children from such humiliation. There's that old American promise again.

Like so many people, we watched helplessly as our life savings were sucked out the door by a world economic meltdown. With only a fraction of our nest eggs left, we were desperate to get our heads above water. For the first time, we feared that our children would be right back where we started—driving old minivans and mowing lawns for Kevin Costner DVDs.

That's when the Dollar Bills entered our lives, like financial angels sent to guide us through a world we frankly did not understand. In the spring of 2010 we each received the same solicitation from a pair of financial experts and entrepreneurs by the names of Bill Richter and Bill Lachey, who identified themselves as "The Dollar Bills." Under normal circumstances, we would've thrown away the junk mail without hesitation. Yet something made both of us open their letter on the same day. Call it coincidence if you'd like. We call it fate.

That very letter is below. Read it yourself, and see if you don't feel moved in some strange way, as we did, to learn more.

DOLLAR BILLS, Inc.

April 15, 2010

Dear Sir or Madam:

As the nation reels and regroups from a recession of epic proportion, investors are anxious and prone to impulsive financial decisions that threaten to bring American capitalism to its knees. The climate is volatile. The circumstances are like nothing we have ever experienced. Investors need a guide. A guide that will lead them to success and prosperity. And a guide that will show them how to look great getting there.

We all know the #1 problem facing Americans today is salmonella. But what people don't know is that the #2 problem facing Americans today is fear. Fear of the unknown. Fear of the financial markets. Fear of ninjas. The result is a blind reliance on the highly flawed strategies preached by the charlatans posing as financial experts on television and in

---

print. We're here to shine a light onto the dark, choppy waters of economic uncertainty and provide you with a new course, due north, to financial freedom. Along the way, we'll teach you to change your perspective entirely—to view money as a seductive mistress instead of a nagging wife.

Sure, we may lack "traditional qualifications" and "any kind of financial, business-related, or college degree," but last time we checked, so does Don Johnson, and he's done pretty well for himself by employing a simple formula of huge balls, a year-round tan, and expensive pastel suits. So ask yourself, do you want to be like Don Johnson, cruising around Miami on a cigarette boat, or do you want to be like the douchebags sitting at home, biting their nails all day waiting to see if Ben Bernaffleck is going to raise the rates again?

The time is now. The choice is yours. We are ready to make you rich. Or you can continue to bite your nails and eat at Long John Silver's. We'll be on Don Johnson's boat drinking Smirnoff Ice, spearing marlins, and Frenching strippers.

We sure hope to earn your business.

Millionairely Yours,

Bill Richter and Bill Lachey
Co-Presidents and CEOs, DOLLAR BILLS, Inc.

While Richter and Lachey's approach certainly seemed aggressive and reckless and their understanding of finance appeared remedial at best, we knew we weren't going to realize substantial returns doing what everyone else was doing. They threw around financial mumbo jumbo we didn't (and still don't) understand, but they shot straight and played from the heart—we trusted them immediately. Something about it just felt right.

So late one night, sipping a couple Red Bull & bottom-shelf vodkas in a dark corner of an off-Strip Las Vegas casino, we agreed to give it a shot. It was time to accept the fact that we needed help in making a better life for our children. When we woke up the next afternoon, we immediately combined our assets and turned them over to the Dollar Bills.

It's too early to say how we've done on our principal investment (plus The Bills always tell us the information is on a "need to know basis"). What we can tell you is that these guys have made an impact on our lives. The education we've received from the Dollar Bills has been the equivalent of a year at Fresno State Business School (that's what they told us anyway). Like The Disciples, we now believe it our responsibility, and our privilege, to spread the Dollar Bills gospel around the world.

The following is a compilation of the strategic materials the Dollar Bills shared with us, for an auto-bill monthly payment of $1,250. They walked us, step by step, through their philosophies on investing and on attaining success across all levels of life. They also encouraged us to reflect on what we learned by jotting down our personal notes at the end of each chapter. The notes illustrate our journey of discovery and our evolution as investors. We hope the information within this book changes your life the way it has changed ours. As Richter and Lachey always say, "You just need the balls to take what's yours and get loaded."

—WILLIE GEIST & BOYD McDONNELL

LOADED!

By
The Dollar Bills
Bill Richter & Bill Lachey

Ready? Let's Do This!!

DISCLAIMER: Do not attempt to execute these complex financial maneuvers without consulting highly trained professionals, i.e., us, the Dollar Bills. Fax us your phone number and we'll call you (collect) to walk you through the specifics and down the golden path to riches.

Testimonials and Praise for the Dollar Bills

"The Dollar Bills tripled my net worth in just 30 days! I'm fairly certain their advice also cured me of the chronic constipation I've battled since I was a child. Thanks, Bills!"

—Matthew O'Brien, Conyers, GA

"I went from living paycheck to paycheck, to making over $250,000 a year without having to leave the comfort of my own living room— and I only had to kill one hobo!"

—Iver Maple, Trenton, NJ

"The Dollar Bills are totally hot! I want them to make me rich, and pregnant!!"

—Anonymous Chick (source not confirmed)

"The Dollar Bills not only got me loaded, they improved my poor hygiene, and my lats have never been bigger!!"

—Ryan Gildersleeve, Salt Lake City, UT

"You know what 'FEAR' stands for? It stands for 'False Evidence Appearing Real.' It's the darkroom where Satan develops his negatives."

—Gary Busey (actual quote)*

*But completely unrelated to this book.

Your Guides

DOLLAR BILLS, Inc.

Dear New Clients Willie Geist and Boyd McDonnell,

Are you ready to change your lives? Enclosed in this package you'll find your guide to becoming a millionaire overnight. Yes, we'll give you all the strategies you'll need to achieve a meteoric rise to power and wealth beyond your wildest dreams, and increase your handsomeness and sex appeal exponentially in the process.

What better way to start than a quote from the work of one of the richest, sexiest men in the history of the world, William Shakespeare:

FORD: If money go before, all ways do lie open.
FALSTAFF: Money is a good soldier, sir, and will on.
—Dialogue from Shakespeare's "The Merry Wives of Windsor"

We've had that quote laminated and clipped to the driver's-side sun visor of our Plymouth Sundances since we strapped ourselves into this entrepreneurialistic rocket ship to the moon in the late 1990s. We literally bought a rocket ship in 1999 with the intention of going to the moon. Then we remembered we both get airsick really easily. The rocket ship is still under a tarp in Lachey's backyard awaiting a buyer who loves adventure. But let's not get off track here.

We'll never know for sure what Shakespeare's Ford and Falstaff were talking about, but what we do know is that achieving financial success, especially in the midst of economic turmoil, is a lot like fighting a war. Today, more than ever, you need a good man next to you in the trenches. As Falstaff's words remind us, money *is* a good soldier. The question is: Do you want it fighting *for* you or fighting *against* you? We can tell you with certainty we wouldn't want to go to war without it (or without a gun and a bulletproof vest. And probably an extra pair of socks and some playing cards).

Within the high-gloss pages of this comprehensive strategy guide, we'll arm you with all you need, not only to survive the war of personal finance, but to dominate the enemy, raise your flag in victory, and return home to a ticker-tape parade. Don't come home in disgrace like the 2004 Dream Team. Come home like Lance Armstrong after he conquered the moon.

—Bill Richter and Bill Lachey, the Dollar Bills

BIOS: BILL RICHTER AND BILL LACHEY, THE DOLLAR BILLS

Bill Richter and Bill Lachey (pronounced "Luh-SHAY"), founders of DOLLAR BILLS, Inc., are among the most widely read* and respected** financial writers in the country. Their biannual column appears exclusively on their personal Web site, and has been forwarded to friends and family members across the country and around the world.[†] Richter and Lachey also host a Web-only investment show called *DOLLAR BILLS* where the longtime friends and business partners answer listeners' financial questions and read sports scores, and do hilarious impersonations of former presidents while waiting for other calls.

On Webcam and in print, Richter and Lachey pass on lessons they learned as successful entrepreneurs. At the ripe age of 27, William "Bill" Lachey dropped out of Phoenix Online University to pursue his dream of opening a year-round laser tag outfit in Seaside Heights, New Jersey. Does that story sound familiar? It should. Bill Gates dropped out of college to start a company of his own. Just swap out Phoenix Online

---

*By their immediate circle of friends/employees/guy at the dry cleaner.

**There's no way to measure respect, but the people listed in the previous footnote don't seem to object to Richter & Lachey's writing.

†They have a budding financial and personal relationship with the Prince of Nigeria, who sent them an e-mail in late 2008 soliciting their help.

University for Harvard and Lachey Laser Tag for Microsoft and we're talking about basically the same thing. Just as they did with Gates, the critics told Lachey his dream was too big. They were right (about Lachey, not Gates). This time.

Meanwhile, William "Bill" Richter was developing an entrepreneurial cache of equal weight and magnitude. At 29, having raised substantial capital from several investors,* Richter began to aggressively dabble in a variety of start-ups and investments, most notably a *Caroline in the City* video game and a combination fertility clinic/dance club. Despite the strength of the ideas, they just weren't hitting. Something was missing.

In 2002, after Lachey had spent two years working the ice cream counter at a batting cage/mini-golf course, fate stepped in, as he was introduced to Richter, who had been playing 54 holes at the course every day. Like so many business partnerships, the first pages of this success story were written on the golf course (mini-golf, in this case). Together, the pair formed the Richter-Lachey Group, with the simple mission of making cash "by any means necessary."

The nature of their business remains a mystery to this day. The Richter-Lachey conglomerate was like Procter & Gamble, Amway, or the U.N.: No one quite knew what it did. The pair leased/rented expensive cars, purchased 1/16 time-

*Over $11,000 in Capital One and Diners Club cash advances.

shares in exotic locales across northwest Florida, and generally lived lavishly as they oversaw a rapidly growing empire that came to include subprime real estate ventures, log flumes and dunk tanks, and a tiny bit of cocaine dealing.

In 2007, flush with cash* and looking for a new challenge, Lachey and Richter had the "how much money is enough?" conversation. They decided it was time to get out of the rat race and begin to share with the world the secrets that made them rich. They founded DOLLAR BILLS, Inc., bought domain names, started writing, and the rest, as they say, is still happening. Now normal people can get a sweet whiff of the success that Lachey and Richter have been chalking up and snorting for years.

---

*There are no records of this income, but Richter and Lachey insist upon it.

Bill Lachey (luh-SHAY) is a native of Scottsdale, Arizona. He was a 3-handicap golfer by the age of 11 and today regularly shoots in the low 70s playing from the pro tees. He is loosely related to Drew and Nick Lachey of the boy band 98 Degrees.*

Bill Richter is a native of Tallahassee, Florida. He once bowled a perfect 100, right-handed. He is an avid stair-masterer. He rises at 3:45 each morning, believing that sleeping more than 3 hours a night displays weakness of character.

*Lachey owns the *Newlyweds: Nick and Jessica* Season 2 box set.

The Bills' Favorites

	Bill Richter	Bill Lachey
Restaurant	Planet Hollywood	Shula's Steakhouse (Orlando Disney location)
Movie	*Tango & Cash*	*Tango & Cash*
Book	*The Art of the Deal* (Donald J. Trump)	*Think Like a Billionaire* (Donald J. Trump)
Athlete	José Canseco	Ozzie Canseco
Vacation spot	South Padre Island, TX	Panama City, FL
Turn-on	Old scotch and new tits	The smell of money right out of the ATM
Turn-off	Kabbalah, yoga, or any artsy substitute for discipline	The smell of poor people
Saying	"FUBAR"	"Who let the dogs out?"
Investment	51% ownership of the AFL team, the Barstow Badgers	The seed money for Joey Fatone's solo album
Hobby	Zebra hunting from a helicopter or Hummer	Buying expensive art and making love on top of it

Section 1

The Economy

Chapter One

A Brief History of the American Economy

They say if you want to understand the future, you'd better study the past. That's great if you like sitting around reading dusty history books that smell like your grandmother's house, but in the world of high finance, only Sallies who drive Japanese hybrid cars look in the rearview mirror. Having said that, a lot of economic losers have been asking the question lately, "How did we get here?" (By the look of things, most of them probably "got here" on the bus.) It's a fair question, I guess, and one that can be answered with a brief, Ask Jeeves- or Google–sourced study of capitalism in America.

Let's start at the beginning, or at least at the part after the Indians conquered the dinosaurs.

From the moment the first explorers (i.e., Columbus, Vespucci, Boyardee) landed on American shores and confronted the native Indians (not the kind of Indians that answer the phone when you call the cable company and pretend they're in the U.S. by asking if you saw the Yankee game last night), the war over the land's dominant economic theory was on. The Indians wanted to trade shitty trinkets like beads, pelts, and sandals—the kind of stuff you buy at dollar stores and throw in the garbage a week later. Meanwhile, the Pilgrims rolled up in their tricked-out boats, carrying tables, rugs, silverware, and fondue sets. We're talking Crate & Barrel, wedding-registry-level stuff.

INTERVIEW OF SAMOSET WITH THE PILGRIMS.

Notice the much higher-quality, higher-thread-count clothing on the Pilgrims than on the Indians. The Indians couldn't even afford real hats!

Dressing for success should be part of every entrepreneur's daily plan. Despite the Indians' lack of style, the Pilgrims were smart enough to see the long-term value of the relationship.

At first, the Pilgrims played along with the lame-ass, bead-trading barter economy, but then they got understandably annoyed and decided to kill all the Indians. Sitting Bull tried to resist but he learned the hard way that, like his people, arrowheads and blowguns were relics of a bygone era. The Indians who survived the epic ass kicking bitched so much about it that the Pilgrims gave them casinos just to shut them up.

From the near extermination of an entire race of people was born a wonderful new economic system. With the Indians out of the way, capitalism was free to take its first baby steps. As Ben Franklin invented electricity, Eli Whitney discovered gin (yum!), and Steve Guttenberg gave the world the first printing press,* American entrepreneurialship took flight. Restaurants, malls, and free-standing sporting goods stores sprouted up all across the vast landscape. As a continent learned to live, work, and speak for itself, the seeds of the American Revolution were being planted right under the King's nose.

George Washington, Thomas Jefferson, and Abraham Lincoln knew the growth of their colonial economy would forever be stunted by the strong hand of the monarchy. That is, unless they did something to change that. In a secret meeting on a cold night in Pittsburgh, a group of brave American men (no broads allowed) played cards, told ethnic jokes, and

*Sometime between *3 Men and a Baby* and *3 Men and a Little Lady*.

Match the Invention to the Inventor:

Telephone	USA
Locomotive	USA
Modern-Day Warfare	USA
Bud Ice	USA
Rockets	USA
Playboy	USA
Football	USA

This was just a drill to prove a point.

The real answers:

Telephone: Albert Einstein
Locomotive: Grover Cleveland
Modern-Day Warfare: Alexander the Great
Bud Ice: Ice-T, in partnership with Bud Light
Rockets: General Patton
Playboy: Hugh Jackman
Football: John Madden

The fact remains, however, that all these people are Americans.

wrote the Declaration of Independence. No one knows for sure what was written in that mysterious document. All anyone can say for certain is that it sparked a revolution.

Within days, Bostonians were dumping their Skim Chai Lattes into the harbor to protest the price of stamps. Witches were being burned at the stake in Salem. And The Million

Man March was stampeding its way to Washington. The mighty British Empire never stood a chance in the face of the American revolutionary spirit. On the 4th of July, King George III called George Washington to concede defeat and the United States of America was born. Celebrations broke out across the young nation (since it was the 4th, people already had shitloads of fireworks and picnic food for celebrating) and the nascent government moved to establish itself as a world power.

In his first act as president, Washington took out a **bridge loan** and ordered that a bridge and toll plaza be built between New Jersey and New York. It was to be named in his honor. But the bridge was much more than a monument to the new president. It opened up the island of Manhattan (which, by the way, some dumb Indian sold to the white dudes for a satchel of beads) to commerce. Soon thereafter, The New York Stock Exchange was built.

ACTUAL TRADE

THIS   for   **THIS**

> **Plain English Guide to Confusing Financial Terms**
> *Bridge Loan:* Leveraging assets (in this case, magic beads) to generate a loan with which to build a bridge. Also applies to toll plazas, piers, and large docks.

If the United States of America was a giant luxury steamship with two swimming pools, a driving range, and a 24-hour sundae bar, the NYSE was the engine room. People bought stocks, bonds, T-bills, triple-tax-free muni bonds, pork bellies, and rookie baseball cards at astronomical rates. Railroads were built, steel companies flourished, and American automobiles became the envy of the world (especially the Chevy Malibu). There was no stopping the American economy. It was the Kobe Bryant of its time.

Later, the Great Depression of the '30s was blown out of proportion by the news media. It seriously was not as bad as everyone says. Even as photographs of tent cities and breadlines were splashed across the front pages of the world's newspapers, capitalism marched forward. Some said the United States was crippled and humiliated by the economic downturn. Really? Hitler, Hiroshima, and the Communists might beg to differ. After kicking major ass in World War II and maintaining its undefeated record in wars, the story of America's military and economic dominance echoed around the world. In 1945, everyone agreed that the United States would run shit. And we did.

WAR RECORDS:

USA	15–0	Top Gun ass kickers
England	0–1	They'll think twice before messing with Sam Adams and the boys again
Germany	0–1	Hitler turned out to be a major douche, and not just because of the weak stache
Vietnam	0–0	This war wasn't officially sanctioned, so doesn't count in the standings
France	0–0	Some may dispute this, but we would argue that France has never meaningfully participated in a war

Since then, we have never relinquished our spot as the world's number one economy. In the '50s, everyone had a car and a house in the suburbs and all the women wore aprons and took their husbands' briefcases when they came home from work. In the '60s, many of the country's youth began smoking hashish, growing beards, and running around naked, but America refused to be dragged down by a small group of hippie troublemakers. In the '70s, the left-wing media made a big deal about a stupid burglary at a hotel in Washington. Obviously no one gave a shit, and the economy continued to thrive. Then came the '80s. The sweet, sweet '80s.

Sometime in that decade, Gordon Gecko starred in a movie called *Wall Street*. He wore suspenders, slicked back his hair, and made shitloads of money. His performance inspired a nation. Overnight, the area where all the money people work was nicknamed "Wall Street." **Investment banks** lined the streets. Raking in cash became a national pastime. Just as President Ronald Reagan predicted, everyone benefited from the mountains of money being made by the guys with suspenders. Most Americans bought European sports cars and houses in the Hamptons. As the world watched the United States with envy (with the help of the international box office success of the *Beverly Hills Cop* movies), it became clear that American capitalism was the only way. The Berlin Wall fell, and the Soviet Union, which had been a house of cards all along, surrendered to the United States. Capitalism's victory was complete.

Plain English Guide to Confusing Financial Terms
Investment Bank: A bank where all the tellers wear vests.

If the international economy was a football game, America was blowing out the world by the end of the '80s. As we continued to pour on the points, the '90s became our end zone dance. With Bill Gates's invention of the Internet and the dawning of the Dot-Com Boom, the United States just flat-out started to embarrass the world. We were up 50 points in the fourth quarter and still throwing bombs. No mercy, baby. Google, bam! iTunes, booyah! Kozmo.com, mindspring.net, what's up now?! The hits just kept coming. Seriously, America kicked so much ass in the '90s, it started to get ridiculous. Incidentally, the two of us bought a few domain names* and got tons of tail during that era.

Recent events in the world economy have led some to suggest that perhaps the American way of doing business is not the *best* way of doing business. Naysayers and those jealous of the success of the United States would like you to believe that the Wall Street coke parties of the '80s and the dot-com nerd bender of the '90s led us to this place. We implore you to ignore such shortsighted hogwash. Remember how all the dorks in *Sixteen Candles* hated Jake, the awesome, good-looking guy who rolled up the sleeves on his button-downs and drove a Porsche? America is Jake. The other countries of the world have always been jealous of our economic coolness and they think this is their time to shine. Sorry, dorks, we're still the good-looking one and we still drive a Porsche. It's always gonna be that way.

They just don't get it. You see, American capitalism has been a wonderful journey. A journey that began when men in blouses and buckled shoes landed on our shores thousands of

---

*Including, but not limited to: www.idrivethegreen.biz, www.letsdothisshit.net, www.runningshit.org, www.sexdrugsandrockandroll.net, www.moremoneythangod.edu.

years ago. Our nation's economic journey, like that of the men on those ships, has been, and will be, rocky at times. Sometimes we'll stray off course when the wind hits our sheets the wrong way. Sometimes the waves of the market will lead us into stormy seas. Occasionally, half the crew will die of rickets after eating halibut that had been left out in the hot, rodent-infested galley for four days. Sometimes some asshole will let his paddle slip into the water and we won't be able to steer the goddamn ship.

Sure, staying home and sitting out the journey on the sidelines is probably safer. It's the easy way. But the American way—the way that has prevailed since the Stone Age—requires you to pack your rain gear (and some long underwear and energy bars), grab an oar, and look to the horizon at an uncharted sea of opportunity. If you trust Mother Nature to guide you to shore, she'll have a bounty waiting for you when you get there. Just watch out for rocks and sandbars. Actually you'll want to park your boat off the coast and take a smaller boat into shore. We're starting to lose track of this metaphor. Just shut up and get in the boat.

DOLLAR BILLS TIP #17

Never drive a hybrid car. It's a sign that you're a whiny tree hugger and not a big hitter. China makes a car that runs on the plasma of baby pandas. Get one.

Willie & Boyd's Notes:

After we read this first installment, we were confused and more than a little skeptical. The Dollar Bills' account of the nation's birth and the growth of our financial system differs slightly from what we studied in high school and college. We contacted them, and, during the call, questioned them on several details, alluding to the idea that they were practicing revisionist history.

After more than a minute of silence on the other end of the line, they responded, "Guys, in case you didn't notice, you can't spell 'revisionist' without 'vision,' can you? So who are you going to believe: a paunchy old history teacher in a corduroy blazer with elbow patches, or two guys with 'vision,' rocking custom-tailored suits worth more than that teacher's annual salary?"

We spoke for several more minutes, and while they never actually answered any of our questions, we did appreciate their passion and their "buck convention" mentality. Ultimately, we agreed that perhaps there's no way to tell, definitively, which version of history is completely accurate, if either. We both went to public high school, so maybe we were the ones who were wrong. And maybe the point is that it's not about the details, but rather, how confident you are in relaying the message.

We talked at length over more appletinis than we could count about whether or not to go through with the Dollar Bills program. The more we talked, the more we felt ourselves buying in. Sure it all sounded a little crazy, but just crazy enough to make us rich.

Chapter Two

A Perfect Storm

(Not the Awesome Clooney Fishing Movie)

Now that you know your history, let's move to the present. It may be decades, indeed centuries, before economists and policemen unravel the complex series of problems that, like the beads of melted alloy on the floor of the steel mill in *Terminator 2*, came together quickly to form a monster that nearly killed us all. Some have called the confluence of factors that led to the near collapse of the world economy "a perfect storm" (and not the awesome kind of "Perfect Storm" when Clooney, Marky Mark, and the other guy from *Talladega Nights* went on a guys-only fishing trip). It was a storm whose thunderclaps of cheap money and inflated profits should have served as warning to all of us. Instead we were caught in the rain without an umbrella. Also, instead of rain, shit was falling from the sky. It was a shit storm. As far as we know, they have yet to make an umbrella that protects you from shit.

In the immediate aftermath of the raging shit storm of the fall of 2008, the American public was given a head-spinning crash course in economics. We heard terms like "subprime mortgage," "credit default swap," "too big to fail," and "you probably shouldn't have bought an Escalade with your Diners Club card" for the first time. Unless you were a regular CNBC viewer, though, this all sounded like Greek (which, incidentally, we speak fluently and use on our fall trips to Athens, Georgia, to see the Dawgs play Mississippi State). Frankly, it's not all as complicated as the so-called "Masters of the Universe" would have you believe. When you cut through the financial mumbo jumbo, the economic crisis can be boiled down to three basic concepts:

1. Wall Street vs. Main Street
2. Bernie Madoff
3. Overpaid Athletes

Let's sink our teeth into these one at a time.

Wall Street vs. Main Street

As we outlined in Chapter 1, Wall Street is the place in New York City where smart, savvy guys wearing monogrammed cuff links and Bluetooth headsets make money by the truckload. Like J. P. Morgan, Cornelius Vanderbilt, and Gerald Ford before them, these men (and the occasional token woman) were the titans of American industry. But like the Tennessee Titans in the playoffs every year, these financial titans totally pooped the bed.

By 1940, just three years after inventing the automobile, Gerald Ford was widely recognized, for obvious reasons,* as the face of American business.

*Most obviously, his business face.

As Bear Stearns, Lehman Brothers, Dolce & Cabana and other places with two names fell like dominoes, the luster began to come off the famous golden statue of a buffalo that sits somewhere near Wall Street (it doesn't come up on Google Maps, so we can't say exactly where it is). Almost overnight, the buffalo's sheen had turned to tarnish. The world financial markets were on the brink of collapse and Wall Street was asking itself some tough questions. Questions like, "Can you believe all these Main Street yokels bought all that shit they couldn't afford and cost us our fucking bonuses? I am *not* renting in Westhampton (aka Worsthampton) this summer."

Wall Street became a popular target for the country's outrage. Suspenders, steak power lunches, and restored vintage sports car collections became, fairly or not,* symbols of the "excess" that helped bring about the collapse. The economic meltdown offered many long-frustrated Americans the opportunity to lash out at people who have beach houses, wine cellars, and home theaters with stadium seating. The unspoken class conflict that bubbles beneath the surface of American life exploded in the fall of 2008 like the volcano at Pompadour. So what *is* Main Street, and why is it so bitter? Simply put, Main Street is home to the people whose irresponsible spending forced Wall Street to make the gambles that screwed us all.

*Unfairly. These assets should all become part of your life portfolio.

Tell us if this sounds like a good idea: Some guy walks up and hands you the keys to a big, five-bedroom house the likes of which you've never been inside (that's what she said). You tell the guy you don't have enough money in your wildest dreams to pay for such a house. The guy tells you that you don't need any money. Just get him back later. No money to buy a house? Sounds weird. Usually things cost money. Especially houses. And sex. So what's the catch?

As long as you're loaded, there is no "catch." In a society, however, where a small percentage of people are not loaded, some bad apples are bound to spoil the otherwise shiny, delicious bunch. In other words, it's the fault of the poor people. The irresponsible Americans who took that sweet housing deal and moved their overweight families (studies show that poor people don't have home gyms or Equinox memberships) into houses they couldn't afford eventually brought the world economy to its knees. Thanks a lot, poor people! Since these dummies previously owned homes that had two bedrooms, they had to buy new furniture to fill up their new "mansions." They had to buy new pool tables for their billiard room. They needed liquor and martini shakers for their swim-up bars. And they had to lease Mercedes to fill up their three-car garages. They slapped all that on their Visa cards and started living the American Dream!

If the Mercedes CL 600 goes in space 1 in your garage, this should shortly follow in space 2. Leave space 3 open for Jet Skis or, if you must, for the Hyundai you currently drive.

It sounds like a dream to us, but the poor people turned it into a nightmare. That kind of spending on luxury goods should have stimulated the economy. Somehow, though, the poor people ruined a beautiful dream. Martin Luther King Jr. famously said in his inauguration speech, "Dreams are made to be broken." Well, Dr. King, your dream has been realized: The American Dream is broken. While Wall Street was rolling up its sleeves and working to maintain the economic supremacy achieved by our forefathers, Main Street was spending money like the party would never end. Homes, cars, custom kitchens, flat screen TVs, riding lawnmowers, single-engine aircraft, home margarita machines, and rare birds were all just a swipe of the credit card away. Main Street's economic fantasy (do you really need a goddamn margarita machine in your basement?) soon became the world's nightmare.

Despite those economic realities on Main Street, Wall Street came under attack by people who don't know shit about finance. They complained that the rich, handsome Bluetooth guys were accepting big bonuses, flying in corporate jets, and filling their offices with sweet antique furniture. We know: So what, right? Executives at financial firms were vilified in the press for living extravagantly as the economy was crumbling around them. Some pundits said Wall Street bigwigs were "out of touch," whatever that means. "Success" became a dirty word. If you had money, you were an asshole. Suspenders even went out of style for a brief period.* The American way of life as we knew it—success, money, and $150 seafood towers—was turned on its head for no good reason.

Cable news, with its unique ability to put the most complex circumstance into professional wrestling terms, labeled the economic crisis "Wall Street vs. Main Street." In one corner, the argument went, we had a group of hardworking, God-fearing Americans just trying to do right by their families (Main Street). In the other corner, a group of greedy,

*One week.

opportunistic financiers willing to cheat and steal to get their hands on the opponent's money (Wall Street). It was like Hulk Hogan vs. Nikolai Volkoff. Good vs. Evil. America vs. terrorists (Volkoff was a Commie terrorist). It all made for a good story and, like professional wrestling, it was all bullshit.

Bernie Madoff

Every good story has a great villain, whether it's *Superman* (Gene Hackman's Lex Luthor), *Superman II* (those three weird outer space people who shot lasers from their eyes), or World War II (Germany's Adolf Hitler). In the beginning, the villain of the financial crisis was the aforementioned "Wall Street." That character proved, however, to be vague and difficult for audiences to sink their teeth into. Plus, the problem clearly was not Wall Street. The script needed a rewrite. America wanted to put a face to the evil. Enter Bernie Madoff.

He is the douche to end all douches. Not the kind of douche who puts a bra on the grille of his car to keep bugs out of the engine. Not the kind of douche who wears five rubber bracelets to show all the causes he supports. Not the kind of douche who puts clothes on his Chihuahua.

No, I'm talking about the kind of super-douche who scams people out of their life savings. The kind of douche who bankrupts your grandmother. The kind of douche who steals $65 billion from his friends and gives Wall Street a bad

Lesser Douches

Madoff has the top seed in douchiness locked up. But there are several other Lesser Douches worth mentioning.

- The douche who wears a shark-tooth necklace. Unless you hand-killed the shark, it makes you look like a girl.

- The douche who wears UGG Boots. See #1 (not sure if UGG comes from a dangerous wild animal, but that's the only way it would possibly work).

- The douche who can't drive the green on a par 4.

- The douche who isn't a member of the Hertz Gold Club. Have fun waiting in line . . . we'll be halfway to the Flagstaff Residence Inn by the time you even pick up your Taurus!

- Dudes who cry. Now, if it is for the sole purpose of getting in some chick's panties, we'll consider letting it slide. Otherwise, you're climbing Douche Mountain without oxygen.

- Vegans/Vegetarians.

- Duke fans.

- The douche who wears a helmet when he Rollerblades. (We roll with no shirts, Umbro shorts, and Oakley Blades. That's it. Always.)

name. Bernie Madoff is a douche the likes of which this world had never seen.

So how did Madoff reach such elevated douche status? Let us explain briefly. For nearly 20 years, Bernie Madoff ran what is called a Ponzi scheme. No one can say for sure what exactly a Ponzi scheme is—it's simply too complicated for most testing models we have available to us. We do know the scheme is named for Charles Ponzi, one of finance's earliest douches. In the olden days (we cannot pinpoint the date of the original scheme, but the photos of Ponzi are black and white so it was probably a long time ago), Ponzi took money from people and told them he was investing it for them. Oh, he was investing it all right—in custom leather shoes and villas on the Italian Riviera (based on his last name, historians assume he was Italian).

When people would call Ponzi to ask how their investments were performing he'd say, "I'm in the middle of something, I'm gonna have to call you back" and hang up really quickly, or he'd crumple up a piece of paper next to the phone and say, "I'm getting bad cell reception, let me hit you back on a landline." Ponzi never hit them back on that landline. By the time people caught on to these evasive phone tactics (which may seem absurd now, but were revolutionary at the time), it was too late. Ponzi was already headed for St. Bart's on a catamaran with sails made of $100 bills.

Bernie Madoff followed the Ponzi model to perfection.

But unlike Ponzi, Madoff had the added accomplice of modern technology to help him pull off the scam. His investors expected not just occasional phone calls, but regular printouts reflecting the performances of their **portfolios**. To satisfy that expectation, Madoff purchased a number of dot-matrix printers—some estimates say he owned as many as thirty-five printers at the height of the operation. Quarter after fiscal quarter, he used these high-tech machines to tell his clients a fictional story of high returns and skyrocketing personal wealth. Sometimes it was annoying ripping the perforated sides off every sheet, but at the profits he was seeing, it was well worth the extra effort. The dot-matrix printouts told the story the investors wanted to hear (except when the toner was getting low). No one asked any questions.

Plain English Guide to Confusing Financial Terms
Portfolio: The folder, often made of rich leather and not unlike a Trapper Keeper, that holds the printouts of one's investments. Allows for easy movement of investments between office, home, and sauna.

Then, in December of 2008, the printers stopped telling the fable. The lie was exposed. Imagine the day you found out there was no Santa Claus and multiply it times 65 billion. That's how shocking it was to the thousands of people and institutions who had trusted Bernie Madoff with their money. When all was said and done, Madoff had lost his clients more than $65 billion. The whole thing had been a fraud. Rich people on the Upper East Side of Manhattan were super-pissed. Thanks to Madoff's decades-long scam, they were forced to *drive* three hours to the Hamptons on Friday nights rather than taking the traffic-free, 30-minute helicopter trip. Many of them were reduced to ordering tap water at restaurants rather than Pellegrino. Tap water, as in the kind that comes from sewers. Some were even seen hailing taxis as chauffeured Mercedes sat idle up and down Fifth Avenue. The horrors were unspeakable, and Bernie Madoff was the bogeyman. He was a villain who made those weird outer space people in *Superman II* look like Cub Scouts (except for the one super-hot outer space chick who had the lesbian fight scene with Lois Lane—he made her look like a Girl Scout).

Overpaid Athletes

When we look back at the decade leading up to the financial crisis of 2008, some of the warning signs we missed seem so obvious in hindsight. Chief among them: the inflated salaries of professional athletes. Just after the 2000 Major League Baseball season, Alex Rodriguez signed a ten-year contract with the Texas Rangers worth $252 million. "A quarter of a billion dollars to play baseball?!" people cried out in protest. The game's purists threw up their hands in disgust. Disillusioned children wept quietly in their bedrooms as innocence spilled, drop by drop, from their virgin eyes. If only someone had done more than throw up his hands or cry in his room like a little bitch. If only someone had done something.

Rodriguez's contract—which we're told was more than the United States' defense budget at the time (we'll have to double-check that, but we remember hearing something to that effect)—opened the floodgates of spending in professional sports and began the crippling of local economies. With taxpayers paying ballplayers' rising salaries (pretty sure that's how it works), a number of city governments were forced to raise taxes, close schools, and suspend garbage collection. No one realized it at the time, but superstars like A-Rod, Manny Ramirez, Bernie Williams, Matt Stairs, and B. J. Surhoff were slowly gutting the U.S. economy.

The cash boom in sports coincided with the Dot-Com Boom of the late '90s and early 2000s, and the mentality was exactly the same: money is no object. The country was, in effect, perpetually "making it rain" in the VIP room we call the United States of America. Five million dollars for a domain name? Why not. Fifty million dollars for a backup second baseman? Sounds about right.

With all the rules of fiscal responsibility out the window, the New York Yankees quickly became the largest company in the United States, just ahead of General Electric and Papa John's (99 percent sure we read that somewhere). As the Yankees continued to grow, they proved one of the fundamental laws of economics: When one entity attains more wealth, another loses it. This is, of course, because there is a set amount of money in the world—if we're getting rich (and we are) someone else is getting poor (who gives a shit). The gap between the "haves" (rich dudes/Yankees) and the "have-nots" (losers/shitty teams) in Major League Baseball grew exponentially (note: This is a good word to use in financial conversations). The national pastime had begun to reflect a society with deep and expanding **socioeconomic** divisions.

Plain English Guide to Confusing Financial Terms
Socioeconomics: The study of poor people being bitter at successful, rich, charismatic people. Also the name of an underground Dutch techno group.

There was a time in this country when baseball, like life, was simpler. The athletes played for peanuts and drank beer with the fans at the local saloon after the game. Fathers and sons huddled around transistor radios to hear every pitch and crack of the bat of their favorite team. Women baked pies and spoke only when spoken to. When baseball became only about the bottom line, the beauty of the game was spoiled. The parallels to the modern economic crisis are unmistakable: In our pursuit of the almighty dollar, we lost sight of what made us great in the first place. Alex Rodriguez, like Bernie Madoff, was the messenger of the end of an era. Here's hoping we return to those days when we played, and lived, for the love of the game. And when women didn't talk so much.

DOLLAR BILLS TIP #29

"Success reads success," as the old adage goes.

Start a Donald Trump Book Club

Begin with Trump's classic, *The Art of the Deal*, and read a different book by The Donald every week. When you get through all of his works, start again.

Trust us, we've been to his office several times. The guy knows what he's talking about. The soles of his shoes are 14-carat gold.

DOLLAR BILLS TIP #30

Seriously, we go to his office like 3 times a week. Just start the goddamned book club!

PS: To emphasize a great point, always fist-bump your boys . . .

. . . and like real players, make sure you blow it up! BOOM!!!

Willie & Boyd's Notes:

Once again, our initial reaction was to question the accuracy of some of the Dollar Bills' information (e.g., Gerald Ford inventing the automobile in 1940? Pretty sure that's off by a few years). But this time, we stopped "sweating the small stuff" and locked in on the message, like Maverick chasing a Russian MiG. For the record, some of their info in this chapter was spot-on: Who would disagree that shark tooth necklaces are douchy? By finding this common ground, and taking more of a "big picture" approach, we felt like we'd finally found our partners in the quest for wealth, power, and spray-tanned abs.

We rushed out to our local bookstore to get started on the Trump Book Club. Unfortunately those titles were not in stock, so we got them on back order from a rare book dealer in the Bay Area. We're currently three books deep into our club. Technically, it's just the two of us, but, as recommended by the Dollar Bills, we refer to ourselves as "a club" to boost the image of importance and prestige. Upon completing each book, we're required to send book reports to Richter and Lachey. Shortly thereafter, they return heavily marked-up copies for us to review and use as learning tools.

We also have weekly conference calls, during which the Bills further critique our interpretation of Trump's books, and our handling of the Trump Book Club franchise in general. Typically, the Bills call us collect for these phone sessions.

They say it's because they're traveling internationally, or hosting an exclusive symposium in a major convention center with no cell service. Not sure what either of those has to do with calling collect, but they've explicitly requested that we not question their tactics. So each week, we just wait to hear from the operator.

Section 2

Your Plan

Chapter Three

The Three Things You Should Do Immediately

Now that you know where we came from (the history part, not the sex part), it's time to lay a quick foundation upon which to build your riches. We're not home builders (we do rent several homes on a month-to-month basis, however), nor do we know the first thing about all the zoning/manual labor that would be required to build a house. But we *are* regularly invited to important events to cut ribbons with oversized scissors and to break ground with golden shovels. Here are three key steps that should be put into action the moment you finish reading this chapter. Don't even take a squirt or anything—do these things immediately.

BE PREPARED

NUMBER 1: Get Bluetoothed

Your very first task is to buy a Bluetooth hands-free earpiece and wear it 24/7 (24 hours a day, 7 days a week, i.e., all the time). Not only does this establish your image as an executive of prestige and power, it says "I can't be troubled with picking up a phone in case of a call." Probably because your hands are too busy fondling a stripper's boobs or manning the steering wheel of your brand-new 1992 Celica convertible. And even if you're just standing in line to order some bagels, it still gives the bagel girl and everyone around you a heads-up that you're a guy to be taken seriously.

Here's some actual dialogue from this exact scenario, which occurred just last week:

RICHTER: "Three poppy seed, two asiago, and wait—is that my phone? No. Okay, two sesame, one sundried tomato."

BAGEL GIRL: "Sure." (But the kind of "sure" that hints at "give me offspring.")

RICHTER: "Sweet. You know what, let's throw in one more sundried tom— (raises hand, indicating "hold on" to the Bagel Chick) Richter, go. Lachey! You old so-and-so! You wanna hit the T-wolves game tonight? I've got courtside . . . you know it! Cost me like two grand each! (glances at Bagel Chick) Okay, I'll have Remington pick you up at seven. Whooo! (back to Bagel Chick) Sorry about that. Yeah, so where was I . . ."

BAGEL GIRL: "One more sundried tomato."

And just like that, she had already done the work for him. When you wear a blinking Bluetooth, people just know they should take care of the little, incidental details while you handle the more important stuff.*

*In this scenario, Richter's phone never actually rang. And that's the beauty of it—you can still get the point across without burning up all your "Nights & Weekend" minutes.

Stay connected *and* impress. This guy is probably hammering out a quick stock option day trade while he finishes lunch. Next up, dessert, i.e., sex with this chick (with Bluetooth on).

In addition to immediate credibility, and a killer look while power-thrusting during sex, Bluetooth technology, when used appropriately, provides you with up-to-the-minute connectivity with current market trends. See a great opportunity to cash out your IRA and buy Tunisian silk? Don't waste precious seconds fumbling with your cell phone when you can just automatically connect to your Tunisian silk broker via your Bluetooth earpiece.

Multitasking is key to success in this digital era. Those who stay one step ahead of the curve do so by multitasking. Bang out an hour on the NordicTrack while listening to this chapter on audiocassette. Read the *WSJ* (*Wall Street Journal*) while getting a pedicure.* Surf some Twits while Tweetering about it. Most importantly, while you're killing all these birds with two stones, always be ready to take that important call. That's called *triple-tasking*, and it's the sign of a true trailblazer.

PROJECT THE RIGHT IMAGE

NUMBER 2: Buy a Boat

Now that you are wearing a Bluetooth earpiece 24/7, you're prepared for any great opportunity. Here is the first of many. We work with people every day who are struggling through the recession—making below-market-value wages, protecting a meager savings, battling enormous credit card debt (which is actually an asset—we'll get to that later in the book), and trying to support their families in the process. And we're telling them all the same thing: Buy a boat.

It's really a no-brainer. Go get yourself a pontoon party boat, stat. Sun Tracker makes a nice 24-foot unit that they can have on the water for you by this afternoon. A pontoon boat makes a real simple statement about you. It says, "I'm a man who has put myself in a position to enjoy plenty of

---

*For the record, we only read *USA Today,* for the pictures. But saying *WSJ* makes you sound successful.

leisure time. And I spend it drinking Mike's Hard Lemonade and eating potato skins on this expensive boat."

We don't want to confuse you with a bunch of our "money-speak," but a party barge is what we call a **floating asset with high liquidity**. That means simply that it's something you own that floats. What it also means is that, in this time of financial uncertainty, while other people are sinking with last generation's ball-and-chain investments, you're sitting, literally, on an asset that allows you to maneuver around the tidal waves of bear markets. Bears, as you may or may not know, are scared of water.

Plain English Guide to Confusing Financial Terms
Floating Asset with High Liquidity: Something you own that floats.

You'll want to name the boat either "Liquid Asset" or "Wet Dream." Yes, these names pop with the confidence of a man who has lots of assets and keeps low overhead and inventory. And that man is you. With the help of a single 25-horse outboard engine, that pontoon boat is a liquid asset that will float you straight to financial solvency.

NUMBER 3: Fly First Class

When you travel with the airlines, always use a flight's first boarding call for "First Class Passengers" even when you're flying coach. Everyone respects a man who travels first class. Stride with confidence through the crowded gate area. Speak loudly on your Bluetooth earpiece about several luxury pontoon party boats you're considering buying. Say you can't believe how ridiculous airport security is and suggest that you may sue the airport just on principle. Carry a briefcase in one hand and precariously but nonchalantly balance your pager and a latte in the other. When you get to the agent, quietly tell her you have a heart condition and you need the extra boarding time. It's important to keep this between you and the agent.

Once on board, quickly make your way to your real seat, 42E, the last-row seat by the crapper, and fall asleep. People who make the connection between the fast-paced entrepreneur they watched with envy at the gate and the snoring, drooling man inhaling urine fumes will most likely just assume that you generously gave your first class seat to an elderly woman and are exhausted from all the deals you've been making. This point is driven home when you land and immediately hop on your Bluetooth to tell your secretary all about it (in a loud, confident voice). Research shows the two things people generally respect most are: 1) tremendous wealth, and 2) helping old people. You've managed to project the appearance of both without breaking a sweat.

Remember, wealth is 80% appearance and 15% money. The other 15% is aged prosciutto and fine Corinthian leather ottomans.

The Breakdown of Wealth

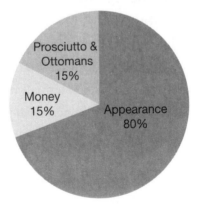

Easy Ways to Improve Your Appearance of Wealth

✓ Go to art auctions. Talk about art. Bored people with a lot of money seem to do that. Lease a Picasso (see if you can do that with no money down).

✓ Travel to Grand Cayman. People assume you're doing highly secret, highly lucrative business in an international tax haven. Stay at the Sandals Resort, 7 Mile Beach, and go parasailing for a few days before coming home.

✓ Erect a gate at your driveway (doing the fence all the way around your house is optional and costly). Put your monogram and/or ornate gold dollar signs on the gate so people know/think a successful businessman lives there.

✓ Invest in thoroughbred horses. The guys at the Kentucky Derby always look rich and they have hot wives with big hats.

✓ Hire a personal assistant and a driver. A businessman isn't taken seriously until he has people around him. A bodyguard is the next step.

✓ Have curtains installed in your car. The very nicest cars have them. Rolls-Royce Phantom, Bentley, etc. You can buy curtain rods and fabric at Home Depot and use a glue gun to put them up around the back seat. When the curtains are drawn on your Saturn, people assume you're a hitter, closing a confidential deal.

✓ Get a Marquis Jet account. Sign up online. Or at least get a Marquis Jet membership card. Or just wear a Marquis Jet hat on the weekends. People will know you own and/or admire private jets.

✓ Hire a world-renowned painter (on spec, if possible) to create a portrait of you, which you can hang in your office and/or cubicle. All successful business leaders have them.

Hire a famous artist to create an expensive portrait of you, to hang in your office or above your bed.

Trust us . . . it's worth every penny!

Willie and Boyd's Notes

We took the Dollar Bills' tips to heart, and the two of us decided to buy a pontoon boat together. Ever since, we've been spending most weekends on Lake Pontchartrain in Louisiana. We stock it with Mike's Hard Lemonade, throw on some J. Geils Band, Doobies, or Rick Derringer, and hit the water.

Again, the early skepticism has been erased—this purchase has had a pretty amazing effect on our image. People seem to look at us with a heightened sense of admiration when we're cruising the protected marshlands, blasting "Rock & Roll Hoochie Koo" and wake-boarding off the back. Admittedly, the wake-boarding hasn't gone too well (the boat mostly just slowly drags us underwater until we have to let go of the rope—Willie's already lost three Bluetooth earpieces as a result), but the overall experience has been very rewarding. People point at us from shore and immediately hop on their cell phones, probably to call friends and tell them about the rich guys they just saw chillaxin' on the sick luxury pontoon boat.

All this mojo, and we've secured a floating asset with high liquidity. Pretty sweet move, Dollar Bills. Pretty sweet.

And the portrait speaks for itself.

Chapter Four

Your Goals

Among all the love affairs, flings, and trips to Asian massage parlors that you experience in your life, no emotional connection is as sacred, and rewarding, as your relationship with money. That's no disrespect to the bevy of Asian massage therapists who have touched our lives through the years, it's just a fact. Your bond with money extends far beyond dollars and cents—it touches and defines the core of your character, the fabric of your dreams, the strength of your legacy. Like anything else of significant value (mink coats, foreign sports cars, 14-carat gold pinkie rings) this relationship must be protected and maintained meticulously. Use the exercises in this chapter as a guide to explore your relationship with money, to define your financial goals, and to unlock the treasure buried deep within you. There are no "wrong" answers, so be courageous and go with your gut.

The first, and most important, question you need to ask yourself is: What do you want to achieve in your life? Do you want to be a successful executive? Do you want more free time? Do you want a Learjet with a shuffleboard court? Everyone has dreams, but what people fail to grasp is the simple fact that money is essential to realizing each of those dreams. Money can't buy you happiness? Whoever said that had clearly never enjoyed caviar and angel dust off a Peruvian hooker's cans while soaking in a saltwater Jacuzzi watching the sunset from a private villa with 700-thread-count sheets on the penguin-down-filled California King mattress.*

Exercise: Setting Goals

Below are two lists of goals. The first list—the WRONG GOALS—shows goals that the "pundits" would tell you are the right benchmarks to work toward. Those are bullshit. The second—the RIGHT GOALS—details the real goals you should strive to achieve—and *will* achieve if you diligently

---

*We haven't actually done this, but we do know that it would take a shit-ton of money to make it happen.

follow our advice along the way. Read these, write them down, memorize them, and burn or eat the piece of paper.

Set Your Goals

Wrong Goal	Right Goal
- I want my monthly income to exceed my monthly expenses.	- I want to lease a Toyota MR2 Turbo with an iPod adaptor and a moonroof.
- I want to pay off my credit cards in full and keep the balances low.	- I want to pay off my credit cards using new credit cards. That way, my old credit cards will be clear for new purchases with the money I saved.
- I want to donate to a charity each month.	- I want to set up a charity in my name to collect **passive income**.
- I want to respect my money.	- I want to make my money respect ME.
- I want to invest $100 per month in a savings account or investment account.	- I want to Jet Ski from Sarasota to Naples, Florida, without stopping.
- I want to save for my child's education.	- I want to make enough money so that my kid never even has to go to school.

- I want to someday buy my own home.	- I want to buy six to nine homes this year with no-money-down, 18-month interest-only ARMs to realize the tax credits.
- I want to work my way up the corporate ladder to a job where I can earn over $60,000 per year and have two weeks vacation.	- I want to stop being a pussy and start making some real "dollar bills" on my own terms.
- I want to pay off my student loans from college.	- I want to sponsor a sorority party at a local university and translate that investment into consensual sex with one or more of the sorority girls.

Plain English Guide to Confusing Financial Terms
Passive Income: Income that gets "passed along" to you from a charity.

Exercise: Fill in the Blanks

Part of the financial journey is getting in touch with your *feelings* about money. Generally, other than feeling amped up, we consider *feelings* to be something reserved for the meek and aimless . . . the lemmings of society. But in this instance, tapping into your feelings—briefly—is an essential part of the journey to financial prosperity. These feelings were likely seeded when you were a child, and that foundation has been built upon over the years to create your perspective today. Here's the bad news: Most of you have the wrong perspective. Here's the good news: There is still time to "shift and drift," just like in the critically acclaimed, Best Picture-winning* film *Tokyo Drifters*. "Shift" into another gear and "drift" around the tough corners of your f—d up psyche. Pretty soon, you'll be burning down the road at Mach 5, smoking all the Korean/Hawaiian dudes you're racing, and getting the hot chick who waved the starting flags to French you in the front seat of your tricked-out MR2.

Shift . . . and Drift!!

The exercise below is structured to help you unlock your money memories, and, in doing so, let them go so you can "shift" and "drift." We've done the first one to help you get the hang of it.

Hi, my name is ____**Bill Richter and Bill Lachey**.
I currently make $____**piles of cash** per year as ____**investment icons and alpha-dog entrepreneurs**. I agreed to have Bill Richter and Bill Lachey represent my financial interests because I want to ____**be somebody who makes it rain in Atlantic City**

*In our members-only movie club.

strip joints. When I think about my childhood, I remember that money made me feel ____**drunk with power**. Sometimes the rich kids at my school said things like ____**you smell like donkey balls, Lachey** or ____ **Richter's scared to shower after gym class because he has no hair on his wiener** and that made me feel ____**like I wanted to make enough money to buy their houses and burn them down**. Today, I (do/don't) ___ **don't** have those same feelings, because ____**when we made our first billion, we did buy all their houses and torched 'em up real good. Unfortunately we forgot that we'd already moved most of our belongings into one of them and I think there may have been a couple cats and/or the owners in another, but that's the cost of doing business**. Today, money makes me ____**a man (and really horny)**. When I feel money in my pocket, I get ____**serious blood flow in my nuts region**.

If I could just get $__**N/A (trick question—we don't believe in banks)** in the bank, I wouldn't have any worries and my life would be complete. I am (certain / confident / hopeful / nervous / doubtful / hopeless) ____**certain** that, with the guidance of the Dollar Bills, I can make this amount of money in the next __**0** to __**0** months **(we're already swimming in it, and so on, and so forth)**.

Ready? Now you give it a try. We added a sentence at the end to motivate and empower you. Remember: SHIFT . . . AND DRIFT!!

Hi, my name is _____

_____.

I currently make $_____ per year as a _____

_____.

I agreed to have Bill Richter and Bill Lachey represent my financial interests because I want to _____

_____.

When I think about my childhood, I remember that money made me feel _____

_____. Sometimes the rich kids at my school said things like _____

__ or _____ and that made me feel _____

_____. Today, I (do / don't) have those same feelings, because _____

_____. Today, money makes me __

_____.

When I feel money in my pocket, I get _____

_____.

If I could just get $_____ in the bank, I wouldn't have any worries and my life would be complete. I am (certain / confident / hopeful / nervous / doubtful / hopeless) _____ that, with the guidance of the Dollar Bills, I can make this amount of money in the next _____ to _____ months. If I am able, I will gladly send 25% in nonsequential bills, via Priority Mail, to Bill Richter and Bill Lachey within five business days.

Signed and guaranteed,

_____ (Your Name Here)

Congratulations! You've now taken the first step toward a fruitful relationship with money. Each morning, prioritize this relationship by repeating this phrase three times:

Today, I am going to get loaded.

"Dirty money" is still money worth collecting, hand over fist.

Don't get caught up in how an investment smells. Just make sure it ultimately smells like money.

For example, we just bought 1,000 of these porta-johns which we're planning to rent to people on a monthly basis as living quarters. Think about it—everyone's talking about "downsizing" these days. Plus, these already come with a built-in bathroom.

Willie & Boyd's Notes:

Wow. Well, apparently we've been approaching our financial goals, and money in general, in completely the wrong way. We've been focused on things like making enough money to cover our monthly expenses, when we should've been saving for the lease payments on a sweet new MR2 with iPod adaptor, or Jet Skiing the coast of Florida. We now realize we've been errantly donating money to charities rather than having the vision to start our own charities and rake in the passive income. Now that we understand what "passive income" really means, this concept is much more clear.

And while we both felt like we had generally healthy relationships with money, by "Shifting and Drifting," we were able to unlock some deep-seeded money memories which had been holding us back. Interestingly enough, like Richter, we too had been chastised in junior high for avoiding the showers, due to being late bloomers. And all this time, we thought we were alone, with no one who understood our painful experiences. So, not only has this chapter strengthened our resolve to establish the right financial goals and build new relationships with money, it has also given us a newfound, deep personal respect for Bill Richter. Our bond with the Bills has never been stronger. Look out, world: The guys with the small, hairless wieners in high school are about to get rich together!

Chapter Five

Developing a Strategy

If you're reading this, you have successfully defined your new relationship with money. No more giggling, hand-holding middle school romance with your cash—now you're banging your money in a rest stop bathroom like a real man. Congratulations. This is the first step toward planting your seed and building your wealth in ways you have never imagined. But make no mistake, there are pitfalls full of vipers between you and that elusive pot of gold. You're going to need the right strategy to swing over the obstacles like a spider monkey on a vine.

Did you know that the average spider monkey has enough strength in its arms to lift a foreign-made midsize SUV clear off the jungle floor? It's true. But raw strength alone is not what made the spider monkey "King of the Jungle." His secret is *vision.** The same can be said for renegade entrepreneurs/handsome investment gurus. It's simple: Devise a strategy and see that strategy through. Just like the spider monkeys. Now it's our job to help you think, and live, like a small primate. In no time at all, you'll have the strength to overturn a

These little dudes can straight up jack some steel in the weight room. But it's their VISION that makes them truly magnificent—in the jungle, and the treacherous world of finance.

*In no way are we suggesting that you should spend fewer than two hours per day at the gym.

Kia Sportage, and the vision to watch its crumpled frame decay below, as you relax with a mai tai, up in the jungle canopy.

Throughout the course of our illustrious careers, we've accomplished and experienced things that 99.7 percent of men can only dream of (e.g., boogie-boarding in Santa Monica with Dane Cook). However, there are few activities that give us as much fulfillment as rolling up our sleeves and educating the average, know-nothing people like you who look to us for guidance. Our goal always is to deliver direct, logical, life-changing advice, and, in the process, establish an enduring, gold-leafed legacy for ourselves. That's how much we care about your success, and our own.

We love to teach people. Here we are at a recent seminar, literally putting money on the screen.

The following transcripts are taken from our internationally syndicated, critically acclaimed, Internet-only investment show, *DOLLAR BILLS*. We trust that you will gain as much from reading these exchanges as the viewers and callers did in real time. We can't really quantify how much they gained because we're not big on "following up," but we're guessing it's in the thousands (millions if we're talking in terms of Dutch guilder). As you read the transcripts, do an exercise (not the Bowflex kind, the brain kind): Think of the variables in your own sad life and about the decisions you would make when faced with these financial dilemmas. Pay attention to the wisdom we spin here and maybe you too will soon be kicking your feet up, pounding premium white zinfandel* while telling off your boss on a wall-mounted speakerphone.

TRANSCRIPT—*DOLLAR BILLS*

Straight Talk Segment: Conventional Wisdom

LACHEY: Welcome to *Dollar Bills*. I'm Bill Lachey.

RICHTER: And I'm Bill Richter. It's time for the Straight Talk.

*From a box, as in, straight from the box.

LACHEY: Yeah, straight. As in, "no funny business." No, seriously, we're both straight. Our job here on *Dollar Bills* is to make you money. Period. If you're an inside-the-box thinker, don't even bother calling in. We live outside the box.

RICHTER: Booyah. Conventional wisdom is for straight-up losers. In fact, if you're anywhere near a convention, you've already lost. Nice nametag, dork. Which corporate master do you work for?

LACHEY: Bottom line: Conventional wisdom plus four bucks will get you a Grande Caramel Drizzled Macchiato at Starbucks. Unless you have a Starbucks frequent customer card and it's your tenth visit. Then the drink is free, but I think you can only get a Tall.

RICHTER: That's right, Lachey. In other words, the value of "conventional wisdom" is zero because a Grande Caramel Drizzled Macchiato is like four bucks at Starbucks anyway. Do the math! Zero! Unless you have the card.

LACHEY: Zero, my friends, is not a number worth investing in. Conventional wisdom would tell you that tight economic times mean cutting back on luxury items. Time to wake up, smell the Caramel Macchiato, and sip some *Dollar Bills* wisdom. There's no smarter time to live lavishly than smack dab in the middle of a recession.

RICHTER: First thing we want you to do: Build a home theater. Stop worrying about your defaulting loans and start focusing on what to charge per head for a *Joe Millionaire* marathon. Stadium seats, Dolby Surround Sound, and ballpark franks don't come cheap. If I may quote Kurt Russell: "If you build it, they will come."

LACHEY: Next move? Go ocelot hunting. Stop worrying about paying your mortgage and start building your future on a lucrative fur-trading operation. Hunting protected wildlife species is the same as printing money. Plus, you get to take a life.

RICHTER: Killing just feels good. Now that you've built a home theater and started an illegal fur business, it's time to invest in a Little League baseball team. It's not about your job of today, it's about your empire of tomorrow. This team of little kids who suck at baseball is just a stepping-stone. Ask yourself: Did George Steinbeck just wake up and own the Yankees?

LACHEY: Of course not. What we're trying to say here, people, is that you have two choices. You can swim upstream and spawn your golden eggs, or follow the masses and float through life choking on the exhaust of lesser men. Not much of a choice if you ask me, Richter.

RICHTER: And if you swim upstream fast enough, you'll soon find yourself in a custom speedboat wearing a sick pair of board shorts and Oakley wraparounds. Just be careful you don't run over the school of weak fish as they study conventional wisdom.

LACHEY: Make mine a cigarette boat with a mermaid painted on the side, Richter! (*excessive laughter from both*)

RICHTER: That, my friends, is the Straight Talk for today. Now go kill an ocelot and hack up a manatee in the outboard motor of your mermaid-painted cigarette boat.

TRANSCRIPT—*DOLLAR BILLS*

Donna in Kansas City Needs a Single-Mom Strategy

RICHTER: Welcome to *Dollar Bills,* I'm Bill Richter.

LACHEY: And I'm Bill Lachey. Today we're going to talk to a single mom trying to make ends meet. We'd like to welcome Donna Fellows to the show. Donna comes to us from Kansas City. She's a single mom working two jobs to provide for her young son, Bill.

RICHTER: Ho! You're halfway there, Donna! Love the kid's name and appreciate the flattering tribute.

LACHEY: Donna, tell us what's going on.

DONNA: Hi, Bill and Bill. Thanks so much for having me on the show, but I have to be honest, um, my son isn't named after you guys. I'm sorry.

RICHTER: Donna, two quick things: 1) It's okay to be a little nervous. This is safe space. We really do appreciate the tribute. 2) I want you to thank yourself, right now, for having the courage to find the answers to your problems. Here's the good news: They're sitting right in front of you.

DONNA: Well, as you said, I'm—

RICHTER: I'm talking about *us*, Donna. We're sitting right in front of you. Probably in HD. Just to clarify. Go ahead.

DONNA: Okay, as you said, I'm a single parent, my son, Billy, is eight years old and he has ADD. I recently had to pick up a second job to cover all the monthly expenses.

LACHEY: What's the primary job, Donna?

DONNA: I wait tables during the day and just started an evening shift at a local movie theater.

RICHTER: Love movies.

LACHEY: You said it. A good Vin Diesel flick, jumbo popcorn, and some Sour Patch Kids . . . tough to beat.

RICHTER: Donna, one crucial question here: Are you happy just to "make ends meet" or do you want young Bill to grow up in the lap of luxury?

DONNA: Well, I mean, I want to—

RICHTER: Simple question, Donna.

DONNA: I want to make a better life, I just don't know how to even make ends meet . . .

LACHEY: Donna, I want you to listen very closely. Get right up next to your computer speakers. Ready? Here's the answer: Hire a full-time nanny. Immediately. American is fine, but European or Italian is preferable. Avoid Central American (Ohio, Iowa, etc.) and German right now.

DONNA: A nanny?

RICHTER: True or false, Donna: Women walking around town with their kid and a hot nanny are usually married to a rich guy. True. Next question, true or false: Nannies give you more time to focus on your revenue streams and disposable incomes. True!

LACHEY: Donna, look at it this way: The nanny only has one job. You have TWO jobs. Do the math, the nanny pays for herself.

RICHTER: Are you following this, Donna?

DONNA: Not in the least. Can I ask a question? All of my friends who are good with money have been telling me to start a 529 account for Billy's education, even if I can only put a little in each month. Can you guys give me some advice on that?

LACHEY: Donna, the only 529 we're concerned with is 5:29 P.M. every day when we blow out of our office and hit Happy Hour at T.G.I. Friday's! Seriously. Unbelievable Thai lettuce wraps.

RICHTER: And two-for-one Goldschläger shots! The liquor with real flakes of gold in it. You're literally drinking yourself rich.

LACHEY: No doubt. But let's get back on point. Donna, you're looking for the next logical step for built-in extra income. And here it is: Become a surrogate mother. Yes, you heard me correctly. You'll get to rub elbows with a classy, upper-tax-bracket couple, which will raise your profile and make you classy through association.

RICHTER: Plus, and this is a big plus, you'll get paid pregnancy leave. And that's when the cost/profits ratio starts looking real good. Much, much better than the ratio on a 529 account. Or, for that matter, any accounts in the 500s.

DONNA: But the restaurant and the theater don't even offer maternity leave.

RICHTER: Well, there's another reason for the nanny, Donna! Problem solved.

LACHEY: Good luck, Donna, give us a call back once you're knocked up.

DONNA: What the fu—

And we lost the call. Our best guess is we will hear from her again, once she's carrying the seed of one of the other waiters. Unless she gets an "indecent proposal" from a charismatic billionaire who comes into her movie theater. Hey, it worked for Robert Loggia and Demi Moore. Who says it couldn't happen to Donna? She did sound rather sexy over the phone—in that desperate, "damaged goods" sort of way. And we love a fixer-upper project. The smell of desperation is so very sweet. So Donna, if you read this, give us a call, let us know where you work—maybe one of us will sire that kid ourselves. Or just bang your hot Swedish nanny.

TRANSCRIPT—*DOLLAR BILLS*

Jerry in Phoenix Needs a LIBOR Strategy

LACHEY: Welcome once again to *Dollar Bills*. I'm Bill Lachey.

RICHTER: And I'm Bill Richter. Let's hit the phones and

start putting some Benjamins in your cargo shorts. Jerry in Phoenix, let's get your problem solved real quick here.

LACHEY: Says here you're having trouble making ends meet around the house, Jerry.

JERRY: No, no. We're doing fine. We *did* talk for a minute about selling our place in Telluride because of this market, but my wife would go nuts if she couldn't spend January up there! And our dog no longer gets a *ten*-ounce filet for dinner. (*chuckles*) But, no, we're good. No, I'm calling because I wanted to get your opinion on some credit default swaps we're considering. Obviously the current climate isn't great, but my company is considering extending CDS contracts to several counterparties. The question is, do I go on the par value and take a physical settlement or do I pay the cash settlement and bank on hitting a low market price of the debt obligation?

(*Silence as Richter and Lachey look nervously at each other*)

RICHTER: Look, Jerry, I don't know how many times I've said this, it's not all about counterparties and CD contracts. Nobody gets laid buying CDs in this market. You may as well dump your hard-earned coin into some municipal bonds. Show me a guy who says muni bonds got him any trim and I'll show you a liar.

JERRY: (*chuckles*) I've been married for twenty years, guys, I don't get laid no matter what I do! But seriously—you and I are looking at the same indicators obviously: issue premium, recovery rate, the credit curve for the recovery rate, and LIBOR.

LACHEY: Well, we can't help you on the marriage thing, Jerry. That's a fundamental weakness in your plan we're not equipped to deal with in this 30-minute show. In terms of LIBOR, Jerry, if I could predict LIBOR for you, I wouldn't be working here. (*laughter from Bills*) Now LIBOR is a funny thing, Jerry. It's one of those economic terms that means different things to different people.

JERRY: Uh, no. It means the same thing to everyone. LIBOR has a very specific meaning. It represents a benchmark interest rate by which banks borrow from one another.

LACHEY: Well I'm sure it does, Jerry. Look, we can sit here all day and quiz each other, but this isn't some high school economics class where we're going to get caught up in terms you and I know damned well aren't on this little test we call life.

RICHTER: And frankly, Jerry, the only "benchmark" you should be focused on right now is getting your bench press max up. From the tone of your voice, I would bet you can barely throw up 185. Poor, Jerry. Poor.

JERRY: What? Okay . . . guys . . . So should I keep my eye on LIBOR, or . . .

RICHTER: Toughest thing in the world to predict, Jerry? The weather. Second toughest? The over/under on a nonconference college football game. Third toughest? LIBOR. I'd rather not talk about it anymore.

JERRY: I'm totally lost. So what do you think? Do I stick to my no-arbitrage "Duffie Model" guns or not?

LACHEY: Yes, absolutely. Duffie is something we believe in strongly. We always say, "If Duffie's selling, we're buying." So, in combination with your strong LIBOR scores, that should be good. And if you look at this graph with all the curves on it, things are looking good. All your charts are strong. All set there.

Offical Quarterly Libor Graph

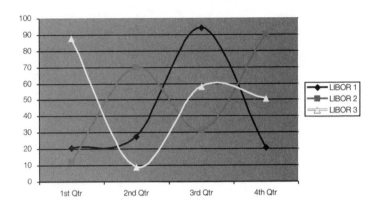

RICHTER: You're all set there, Jerry! It's a win-win. A loss leader. Also, "invest in China."

JERRY: I can't even remember what we were discussing. It almost seems like you guys have no idea what you're talking about. What kind of business did you say you ran?

LACHEY: We can sit here comparing résumés all night, Jerry, but we'd rather you take that LIBOR and start building a five-car garage filled with the fruits of your labor. Talk is cheap. DeLoreans are not.

JERRY: I'm reporting you idiots to the SEC. Goodbye.

RICHTER: Thanks, Jerry. Old fashioned world of mouth is still our greatest marketing tool. Thanks for spreadin' the word.

We haven't heard back from Jerry. He's probably been too busy studying his glossary of confusing financial terms. We can only assume he followed our advice and is now relaxing in his new five-car garage. Jerry, if you're out there, and still think being married is the right move, we at least hope your **LIBOR** investments and Chinese venture capital maneuvers are getting your wife to finally give you sex—on the hood of your new DeLorean.

Plain English Guide to Confusing Financial Terms
LIBOR: Lateral Investment Buyouts and Outsourced Revenue. (Don't worry about what it "means"—technically it has never been defined—just remember to keep your LIBOR scores up)

We hope you found these conversations as helpful as our guests did. To recap the first steps toward developing your strategy:

✓ Think like a spider monkey.
✓ Don't sit in the sinking "conventional wisdom" boat when you can hop into your very own cigarette speedboat with a topless mermaid painted on the side.

✓ Get a European or Italian nanny. Even if you don't have kids, a hot nanny will allow you more time to focus on your strategy.

✓ Keep your LIBOR scores strong, and when in doubt, do what Duffie does.

✓ Try to incorporate a DeLorean into your 6- to 12-month plan.

DOLLAR BILLS Tip #132

Buy a top-of-the-line gas grill with the optional rotisserie function. This lets your neighbors know you're "living the dream" and is also a great place to hide $50–60K and precious metals in the event that you sense you're being observed by a government agency.

Willie & Boyd's Notes:

We followed Tip #132. We each bought the most expensive grill on the market. We have yet to hide large amounts of cash in them, but that doesn't mean the tip isn't working. In addition to surprising our wives with delicious rotisserie chickens and grilled zucchini, we have noticed that our neighbors are more than a little impressed. Richter and Lachey always preach the value of what they call "multi-platformity," and this, they say, is an ideal example, what with the main grill and then the raised rack for shrimp and veggies. Totally awesome.

We also tried to start an ocelot farm, but it was quickly shut down by local, state, and federal authorities. We spent nine months in the same prison where they sent Michael Vick. The good news, we sold enough cigarettes in the slammer to buy a Little League team, just like the Bills said we should. (They attribute our success here to our spider monkey–like vision and strong LIBOR scores.) The team's hovering right around .500 and we're not hitting very well with runners in scoring position, but we are charging the parents two grand for season tickets to watch their own children play. Thanks, Dollar Bills!

Chapter Six

The Three Things You Should Do Immediately, Right After You Do the First Three Things We Told You About Earlier

PRACTICE SMART BUSINESS

NUMBER 1: Buy an Exotic Pet

We recently participated in a live online chat with our fans. The following is a transcript of that chat which will let you in on one of the smartest tactical maneuvers you can make in this volatile market.

RICHTER: We've been flooded with Internet chat e-mails tonight. Lot of uneasiness out there right now. What are they saying, Bill?

LACHEY: I've got an Internet chat e-mail right here from Janelle in Costa Mesa, California. She writes, "Dear Bills, I'm nearing retirement age and this crazy stock market has me scared to death that my savings are going to be wiped out before I get there. What's your advice?"

LACHEY: Janelle, appreciate the chat. There are millions of people in your position right now. But now you're going to know the secret they don't: Buy an exotic pet.

RICHTER: BOOM!

LACHEY: Why do I say that? Two things: prestige and resale. If you own a Siberian tiger cub, people assume you're an eccentric millionaire. As you know, we always preach that it is every bit as important to APPEAR rich as it is to actually BE rich.

RICHTER: You know who else has tigers? Super-wealthy oil sheiks from Arabia. Those tigers live in palaces. Would you like to retire in a palace, Janelle? I sure would.

LACHEY: Now why do I bring up resale? Because buying a giant Siberian tiger is an investment. I once bought a rare African albino crocodile for $32,000 and flipped it the very next day for $32,500. Don't get attached to the animal, Janelle. It's nothing more than a pile of cash with striped fur.

RICHTER: I have a couple of tarpon living in my infinity pool in Coral Gables, Janelle. Wanna make a splash with clients and professional investors? That's a pretty quick way to do it.

LACHEY: Janelle, buy an exotic pet. I don't care what it costs. It's just smart business.

5 Smart Exotic Pet Investments to Make Today

Poison Dart Frog: Endangered Status. Touching with bare skin can cause death. Talk about a flashy investment!

Snow Leopard: Endangered Status. Incredibly soft and gorgeous coat (and/or hat) can be made from its incredibly soft and gorgeous fur. Great around kids and other cats.

Black Rhinoceros: Endangered Status. Poor eyesight means constant supervision is needed in tight spaces and around home valuables, but otherwise harmless and fun to ride.

Whale Shark*: Vulnerable Status. This shortcoming in status is more than made up for by sheer size and "wow" factor. Remove all rafts and volleyball nets from pool before delivery.

Gharial: Endangered Status. Over 2,500 razor-sharp teeth. It is recommended that gharials be kept outside.

*Photo by Zach Wolf.

NUMBER 2: Start a Ponzi Scheme

Start a Ponzi scheme. Now is the time. Forget what we said before about Madoff being a monster-douche and just start the freaking Ponzi scheme. They're not going to be looking for it again after it just happened. The same liquor store is never robbed twice in the same week, right? Lightning never strikes the same place twice, right? Baseball players never hit home runs in consecutive at-bats, right? Women never get pregnant twice in one year, right? There's never been a better time to start your own Ponzi scheme. We're unable to provide details on how to execute this plan at the moment, due to ongoing investigations and a potential wiretap/FBI tail, but our suggestion would be to just put the wheels in motion, and figure out the rest later.

NUMBER 3: Open a Restaurant with a Celebrity

Anyone who tries to tell you that the restaurant business is risky is right, but there are two big caveats: 1) This person is a pussy and should not be trusted, and 2) This person isn't smart enough to solve a simple equation:

> Fancy food
> + A big name
> + Red-carpet opening
> + Interest-only loan
> = Successful eatery

Most people fail in the restaurant business because they try to open bistros and cafes based on cooking talents, location and good critical reviews. That's like trying to win the Olympics by training nonstop for four years. It's a load of horse poop. In the world of restaurants, it's all about making a splash. And that is done through four simple steps.

Step 1: Team up with a celebrity. Landing a big name, like Mindy Cohn, Grant Show, Marcia Clark, or Edward James Olmos, will give your venture the heavyweight status you need when you enter the ring.

Step 2: Food. Here's a little secret: Success in this business has virtually nothing to do with the food. You will prevail by employing the tried and true formula of big plates, small entrees, and calligraphied, leather-embossed menus filled with fancy/foreign words (balsamic reduction, micro-greens, encrusted, succulent, Dover sole, etc).

Step 3: Secure an interest-only loan. Better yet, have the celebrity do it. That way, if/when the restaurant goes belly up after three months, you won't have to deal with the whiny bankers.

Step 4: A HUGE opening. Red carpet, limos, paparazzi, confetti, and fireworks are must-haves. Dramatically unveil an enormous saltwater aquarium in the middle of the restaurant. Fill the place with high profile socialites and kick back at the bar with Mindy to enjoy the first of many celebratory Cosmos. This is going to be a fun ride!

Take some risks!

In order to hit it big, you've got to be comfortable taking risks. Here, we're going for the jackpot, but in doing so, we're not only risking the dollar we put in the machine, we're also risking that the Pechanga Casino and Resort security will, once again, catch on to our "slot counting" scheme.

(Our scheme is a lot like that movie about the MIT card counters, but without all the fancy math. Plus, we get much more tang than those nerds.)

Willie & Boyd's Notes:

We marched out to the nearest black-market exotic pet broker and bought a poisonous dart frog the moment we finished this chapter. Little did we know (nor did the Bills warn us) that this little guy could really jump—right out of the jar we were planning to keep him in. It's been four days and he's still loose. We can only assume he's roaming the house . . . waiting to make a kill.

To make up for lost momentum, we've put calls into several celebrities to see if anyone is interested in opening a swanky new restaurant with us. So far, we haven't had a lot of luck—after our first solicitation, Billy Zane classified our e-mails as SPAM, Tracey Gold's voice mail is always full, and by the time Willie finally tracked down Ryan Leaf, Leaf said he had already committed to opening a little tapas joint in Colorado Springs with Judd Nelson. That said, we're determined to make this work, so we've gone ahead and put down a nonrefundable deposit on a 350-gallon saltwater aquarium and twelve baby blacktip reef sharks. Like Richter and Lachey said, you gotta take some risks to win big!

Chapter Seven

Four More Things You Should Do Right Away, After You Do All That Other Shit We Told You to Do (Seriously, These Are Also Very Important)

START THE RIGHT HABITS

NUMBER 1: Golf

Did you know that 87 percent of people who are in the 90th percentile of success golf at least three times per week? It's true. Not only does golf provide a wonderful excuse to wear sweater vests, the golf course is an ideal place to network, talk business, and consummate mergers and acquisitions. Here are several key tips to help you prepare for hitting the links, even if you never actually hit the links.

1. Join a private, exclusive country club. (Do a social membership only—costs less. Then get others to pick up the greens fees.) Special note: You can't do this one if you're black or Jewish. You'll likely be relegated to public par-3s with women and non-European foreigners. But if you're blond with high cheekbones and a proper upbringing, the country club step should be a layup.

2. Always be practicing your golf swing. Downtime in the office? Take a couple hacks. Brainstorming with your team in the conference room? Walk the room and swing while you think. Even better, get your secretary to stand by, pretending to be your caddie. Pumping gas? Work on the short wedge. Airport ticket counter? Simulate a scenario where you're in a sand trap. And so on. No clubs needed. Just start practicing.

3. Tell stories about your recent or best rounds. Trust us, this stuff never gets old. People will be on the edge of their seats as you regale them with suspenseful tales of how you fought your way off the beach and double-bogeyed 14 at Shady Pines in Jackson, MS. In general, pepper your conversations with references to steak,

cigars, and Phil Mickelson. This will give you serious cachet, and will simply make you more appealing.

4. Get your wardrobe "up to par." Give the jeans and T-shirt to charity and replace them with a nice collared Callaway golf shirt and some Ralph Lauren pleated khakis. Some whale-printed Croakies will complete your new look. Feel free to accent your outfit with pagers and cell phones hooked to your belt (particularly if those devices are synced to your Bluetooth earpiece).

Get these four steps in motion, and you'll be ready to run with the big boys* in no time.

NUMBER 2: Go Green

In case you haven't noticed, people are really into "green" things these days. This trend is largely a hoax created by Hollywood, the liberal media, and Al Gore in order to scare people into believing that something called "global warming" is going to kill everybody. Sounds like the plot of *Armageddon*, if you ask us. That said, we're here to play the roles of Affleck & Damon . . . to drill down to the core of this issue (that's what she said) and show you that if you dig deep enough, there is a way to uncover a big-time Hollywood payday *and* get the girl.

---

*By "big boys," we do not mean Seve Ballesteros, Geoff Ogilvy, and Padraig Harrington. We mean the heavy hitters in your office and/or town.

Look, we would never tell you to actually waste all your time wearing patchouli, going to Earth Day, and sorting paper and plastic—but the fact is that the government is basically handing out money to people and companies that do "green" things. With a couple creative maneuvers, you can take advantage of the emotion around this issue and turn it into the only kind of paper that matters—the kind with presidents' heads on it.

Our recommended course of action here is to start a green charity. Spread the word that you're researching alternative energy sources, or saving enough cardboard to build a town. These are the kind of hot phrases and environmental buzz words that will get the government coffers open. All this stuff is so intangible and unquantifiable at the moment, you should be able to get substantial grant money with very few questions asked. Nobody really knows for sure what constitutes "alternative energy" yet, so just keep it short and sweet when you call your congressman. Here is an example of how this type of phone conversation could unfold:

YOU: Hello, Congressman Hollandaise, it's Ned Feathers (use a fake name that sounds "environmental") calling.

HOLLANDAISE: Yes Mr. Feathers, what can I do for you?

YOU: I want to talk to you about some alternative energies and carbon neutral solutions I've been working on. I think this could be really big for the local economy. I'm pretty close to a huge breakthrough, but my funding is running out. I've put all I have into green research, and I need roughly another $350,000 cash by COB today to get there.

HOLLANDAISE: Sounds interesting. What kind of alternative energy are we talking about here?

YOU: With all due respect, Congressman Hollandaise, I think we've been doing pretty well so far with you handling the Congress stuff and me saving the planet. Let's not fix what isn't broken, yes?

HOLLANDAISE: I'm sorry?

YOU: Mr. Congressman, you're up for renewal soon, right?

HOLLANDAISE: Reelection?

YOU: This thing could be your ticket. Your hot-button issue. We can sit here all day going back and forth about semantics, or we can change the world together. PS: Green.

HOLLANDAISE: The money will be wired to you this afternoon. I have your vote, rig—

And you hang up. From there, just put together some fiscal reports every so often to send over to old Hollandaise. Trust us, he'll be so busy hammering the talking points about your new energy plan in his campaign that he won't have time to figure out that you're in Daytona Beach buying a controlling position in the local airbrush/tank top market.

Forget the fancy meaning the hippies have ascribed to this symbol. It's not of your concern. Follow our "green plan" and soon the greenbacks will be circling around *you*.

CHALLENGE AND SURPRISE YOURSELF

NUMBER 3: Bury 25 percent of Your Money

Huh? You heard us. Bury 25 percent of your money in an unknown location. Today. Why? Ever hear of the term **"found money"**? It refers to money that you find, on the street, or in a hidden spot, and it's the best kind of money there is, because you didn't expect it, and it can boost the shit out of your bottom line.

> **Plain English Guide to Confusing Financial Terms**
> *Found Money:* Money that you find on the street or in a hidden spot; the best kind of money there is. Not to be confused with "stolen money." That's the stuff you score when you siphon cash from your niece's Girl Scout cookie sales.

Plus, by hiding 25 percent of your net worth, you'll be that much more motivated to turn the remaining 75 percent into 100 percent. When things come too easily to people, they tend to get lazy and start dropping the ball. Laziness breeds failure. Challenge yourself! Burying 25 percent of your money in a secret place forces you to not only work harder to make up the lost funds, it forces you to look for it as well, which will exercise your "think muscles." This will carry over into various aspects of your life, but none more obviously than your financial life. Powerful "think muscles" will give you the upper hand in negotiations, allow you to quickly assess complex investment opportunities, and, in some cases, may enable you to see the future.*

Yet another good reason to bury some of your money in an unknown location is that, just in case Russia invades our country again, you'll have some crisp coin stashed up in the mountains that you can use to get AK-47s and RPGs and grease all the Commies. (Ask yourself—who was more prepared the first time around: the Wolverines in *Red Dawn*, or

*This has never happened—yet.

Anne Frank? Last I recall, all Anne Frank had were some stale bread crumbs and a couple shitty candles.) So, on second thought, create a map to lead you to your buried money. But bury the map in a different secret location. And make it one of those awesome road maps with the dotted lines leading you to the treasure. Oh, and definitely burn the edges of the paper to make it look like an old-fashioned pirate treasure map. Damn, this is gonna be fun!

NUMBER 4: Double Down on 13

Go to the nearest blackjack table immediately and double down on 13. Why? You'll catch people by surprise, and surprise is the next best thing to certainty. Remember—people love surprises. Surprise birthday parties. Surprise endings to movies. Finding a clown living in their attic. This same theory holds true in the world of making money. Double down on 13, and everyone at that $10,000 minimum table, including the dealer, wonders what you know that they don't.*

Could it end badly? Sure. Welcome to the world of high-stakes finance. If you can't handle that possibility, what the hell are you doing in the casino in the first place? Exactly. Because we told you to go there. Just double down and take your winnings—and the chicks you've just impressed—to *The Criss Angel Show* immediately.

*The same theory goes for hitting on 18 and splitting 3s.

Other Opportunities for Surprises

✓ Wear all black and a ski mask into the bank when you make your next deposit. They'll be shocked to find that you're not trying to rob the place at all, but rather you are experiencing a visibly grotesque reaction to a chemical peel and must avoid all sunlight. Hey, you never know, they may waive your transaction fee.

✓ Go to a Hollywood hot spot and make it rain with $100 bills. You'll definitely be the center of attention, and you never know who might be there. You just might find that big name for your new restaurant idea. (This can get pricey if no celebrities are on site for several hours/days, so time it strategically—and speaking from experience, Planet Hollywood, despite the name, is not all it's cracked up to be for this approach.)

✓ Wait in the back seat of a prominent executive's car. In today's job market, it's nearly impossible to get enough "face time" to make an impact. Six to eight hours later, when he gets in to drive home, and you pop up clutching a gold letter opener (to open the envelope with your résumé in it), you're sure to make an impression that will move the needle.

One last point—just as important as understanding the key habits to employ today is identifying the various pitfalls that exist between you and victory. Below is a list of five things you should avoid like the plaque (name a single billionaire with bad oral hygiene):

Five Things You Should Never Do

1. **Never follow "the rules":** This will get you about as far as the douchebag sitting next to you on the bus. Breaking "the rules" and writing your own, new rules will get you off that bus and into a new, pre-owned Miata convertible. Now *that* rules.

2. **Never sit while speaking:** When in meetings or negotiations, it is crucial that you stand while you are speaking. This projects an air of confidence and power. You're physically, and literally, above the other person, and they'll feel this superiority, whether they know it or not. So when it's your turn to speak, stand up and look down at your adversary.

3. **Never allow someone to speak more than you do:** When in meetings or negotiations, you should speak at least 76 to 80 percent of the time, leaving only a handful of brief opportunities for the other person to talk. This will show him/her that you have the most knowledge and deserve to be respected and rewarded as such.

4. **Never use a bill lower than a $20:** In fact, it's good practice to only use $50s and $100s. If there's change, leave it, telling the person who serviced you to "go buy something nice for yourself." Being seen with $10s, $5s, and God forbid, $1s, will tell people you're a second-rate executive—a bottom feeder. Be a hitter.

5. **Never trust a cat owner:** Duh!

Don't be afraid to get in bed with exotic investors.

Literally.

Sometimes you have to sacrifice something to close the deal. For example, we had group sex with this wealthy Swedish financier. We did it for the deal. We love chicks (obviously).

Willie & Boyd's Notes:

While we've never actually had group sex with a Swedish guy to get a deal done, the Dollar Bills' point is valid—sometimes you have to give to get. You've got to be willing to compromise in some way to reach an agreement that works for everyone. This is lost on many people, who can't seem to pause or listen long enough to see what the other party needs to feel complete. In this case, yes, Richter and Lachey take the idea to the extreme, but then again, they're filthy rich as a direct result of their instincts. And the Swedish financier likely feels equally compensated. Lesson learned, Dollar Bills. Teach on.

Once again, we've embraced the Dollar Bills' tips in earnest. Yesterday, we simulated an entire 18 holes while waiting in line at the DMV. For over an hour, we dramatically crushed balls off the tee, worked off the rough, blasted our way out of sand traps, finessed birdies, and guided 40-foot putts to the hole. By the time we arrived at the window, we were sweating profusely, and on our fourth Bud Selects. To our surprise, the representative was not interested in our tales of heroism. In fact, she immediately went on break and never returned. DMV Lady: 1, Willie and Boyd: 0. But we can guarantee you, we'd smoke her on the back 9.

Section 3

Your Investments

Chapter Eight

Invest like the Best, Only Better

We ask people to think of investing like a day at the zoo: You can go home happy with a belly full of cotton candy and a few stories about those silly penguins or you can fall into an enclosure and be mauled by a bloodthirsty polar bear. Most investors are satisfied with the penguin stories, and who can blame them? It's the safe, easy way to invest. Big-game hunters like us, though, want to tangle with the polar bear—and you'd better believe we're coming home from the zoo with his pelt for a sick rug to put in the den under our vintage *Cannonball Run II* pinball machine.

There's been so much fear and hysteria whipped up need-lessly by the media over the last few years about the dangers of investing in a home, in the stock market, or in a private jet. Sure, it's scary out there, but we're just glad that, way back when, the revolutionary colonists didn't surrender at the first sign of danger with the British. Otherwise, we'd all be speaking German right now (don't quote us on that until we can double-check, but it sounds right to these two Herrs). Forget what the gutless sissies in the press are saying—they don't care about you. We do. The Dollars Bills are here to tell you: It's safe to go back in the water (and we should know about water safety because one of us was a lifeguard at the Six Flags over Texas wave pool for a summer and the other owns the 30th anniversary collector's edition DVD of *Jaws* with all the extras).

The investment advice you're about to read bucks today's bedwetting conventional wisdom by daring you to put down the cotton candy, walk away from the kiddie petting zoo, and dive into that polar bear cage where the real money is made. The risk of having your limbs torn off by a savage killing ma-chine is pretty darn high—we'll grant you that. But just think about the rewards if you survive: Somebody's getting the key to the city and a spot on the late local news! Let's dive in and slay that bear before he goes off on another whiny rant about his ice caps melting.

Owning a Home

Well, this is where the so-called "problems" all began: the housing sector (note: "sector" is a vague term that makes you sound smart. Tack it on to the end of any noun to impress clients and friends, e.g., "Did you save room for the dessert sector of the meal, Doug?"). You didn't know it but your beautiful home—the place you saved and saved to own so at last you could have a family sanctuary filled with the laughter of children—was, in fact, a deadly cell in the cancerous tumor that almost killed the American economy. That's right, the government and the media (one and the same, if you ask us) say it's YOUR fault, America!* They say you reached too far for that American dream. They say you were irresponsible for accepting loans that required you to pay only in Garbage Pail Kids trading cards for the first five years. Here's what we say, America: You're not taking the fall for these dicks.

By now you've heard all the scary terms: **"foreclosure,"** **"subprime mortgage,"** and **"predatory loan."** Excuse us, but the last time we checked, predators were the biggest badasses of all (e.g., alligators, lions, Schwarzenegger/ Ventura/Weathers in *Predator*) so explain to us again, if you would, how "predatory" loans are a bad thing. That's what

*Yeah, we know we said that too, earlier in the book, but it's good for business to pretend, from time to time, that you give a shit about Main Street.

we thought: There is no explanation. You see, the-powers-that-be are trying to frighten and confuse you like you're at a midnight showing of *The Blair Witch Project*, which was frightening and confusing because we didn't get the ending. I mean, did you? There's only one way to fight back against their dirty *Blair Witch* tactics: buy more houses and prove 'em wrong!* Do these geniuses think we're going to get out of this recession by *not* buying assloads of houses?! We're no Century 21 agents (although we'd kill for a couple of those gold blazers), but we're pretty sure that makes no goddamn sense.

Plain English Guide to Confusing Financial Terms

Foreclosure: When some guys from the bank come to help you move out of your old place into a sweet new loft with exposed brick walls.

Subprime Mortgage: Money lent for investments in nuclear submarines and other prime underwater submersibles.

Predatory Loan: Loans made to predators (e.g., cheetahs, crocodiles, jacked dudes with brass knuckles, and, most importantly, savvy entrepreneurs).

"Easier said than done," you say. Fair point. To that we respond, "Stop being a pussy. You're embarrassing yourself."

---

*That, and never, ever camp in an area that could be classified as "off the map," "a place where compasses literally stop working," or "a great place for a bunch of heinous murders."

This weekend, if you can take a break from watching the LPGA and tending to your vegetable garden, we want you to pick up the newspaper classifieds and find the five most expensive houses for sale in your area. Some "new media" types suggest you do this on the Internet. They forget to "suggest" to you that going on the Internet is a great way to have your identity stolen. Thanks for the advice, but we think we'll risk getting a little newsprint on our fingers to stay away from your rip-off scam, dot-com douche.

Back to business. Start at the most expensive house on the list, call the Realtor listed, and make an offer of $50,000 over asking price, sight unseen. Want to make a splash in the housing market and spark the fire that will turn this economy around? Bid high and let 'em know you're a player. Before the agent can respond to your brazen offer, inform her that you want the current residents out by the end of the week or there's no deal. This aggressive stance achieves two things: 1) It establishes you as a baller, and 2) It gives you a nice hedge against your claims of being a baller because they'll never be able to move out that fast and you can walk away from the deal without actually having to buy the house. You may not have that split-level home with a koi pond, but you've served notice that there's a new market shaper in town. Imagine the respect you'll be extended by the real estate community later, when it actually comes time to buy a house. They'll practically hand you the thing for free!

One other note: You should call in the offer from one of those disposable cell phones that street dealers, cartel henchmen, and terrorists use. The last thing you want is for them to call you back accepting the offer. Then what? Wear latex gloves when you dial the Realtor and throw the phone down a sewer when you're finished with the call. It sounds odd, but it actually looks cool—like something Jason Bourne would do.

If, for some reason, you do find yourself wrapped up in a contract for a house you can't afford, just call one of those "free money" 800 numbers whose ads they show at 3 A.M. during *American Gladiator* marathons on ESPN Classic. We've heard especially good things about the one Montel Williams endorses. They'll hook you up with the cash you need to get started and, who knows, you just might win a chance to meet Montel!

If none of this works as you pursue your dream house, just get one of those kick-ass predatory loans from the bank. They're the bomb!

The Stock Market

Talk about scary and confusing! The stock market has been just about the scariest and most confusing place in the world lately—if you're a complete pussy. Allow us to take the mystery and motion sickness out of what the media fear mongers call "a roller-coaster ride." Once again, we must have missed the meeting where we got together as a nation and suddenly decided that roller coasters are not the most awesome thing ever. As Lachey always says about the Great American Scream Machine, "The drops are the best part!" Indeed, half the fun of the stock market is losing all your money in one dramatic plunge. All you can hope for is that they caught you with a crazy face on the Coaster Cam so you can purchase the photo on your way out.

If you only want to ride the kiddie coaster, this book ain't for you. You must be *this* tall to ride with the big dogs!

The first thing we preach about the market is not to get caught up in the confusing terminology. What's a stock? A bond? A T-bill? A mutual fund? Who's Charles Schwab? We'd rather not treat you like fifth graders trying to memorize words for a Social Studies quiz. It's not the terms that matter. It's the cash that counts. If you've seen the movie *Trading Places* you know everything you need to know about markets and trading. All those guys in the blue barber coats screaming into two phones and waving pieces of paper are the ones who do the work. Those are the guys who have to know what the words mean. You're busy enough as it is shopping for Sea-Doos and hammocks.

Forget the homework and trust your instincts. We find that our highest returns come when we study the least—so, simply put, go with your gut. If you see a sweet car cruising down the street, find out who makes it and call in a "buy" order to one of those guys who yell on the floor of the exchange with the two phones. We did that a few weeks ago when we saw a super-ripped guy just killing it in a Mercury Sable at the Sonic drive-thru. We immediately picked up our car phone and bought a hundred shares of Mercury Sable. Every broker is different, but with our guy we just leave a phone message and our credit card number on an answering machine. He says person-to-person contact could "compromise the investment," so we've never met or talked to him, but as we always say, it's important to take the long view on investing. We'll check in with him in ten years when these bets are really paying off big! Again, let the number crunchers and paper wavers handle the minutiae. Your job is to think big, and let the roller coaster do the rest.

Another technique the people at CNBC, Bloomberg, and other know-it-all business channels use to tie your brain in knots is to show you confusing charts with squiggly lines. Nice try, financial media: We're not impressed by graphs that look like something a two-year-old scribbled while sitting in a pile of his own poop. There are few things about investing we can tell you that are more important than this: *Trust pie charts and pie charts only.* They're round, colorful, and easy to read. Do you think it's an accident that *USA Today* is America's number one paper? Two words: pie charts. Just the other day *USA Today* had a pie chart that showed only 19 percent of Americans say broccoli is their favorite vegetable. Did you know that? We sure as hell didn't—until we saw it in a pie chart. So the next time some yahoo on TV starts yelling at you about a squiggly line graph and what it says about a stock price, change the channel and go steam some broccoli.

America's Favorite Vegetables

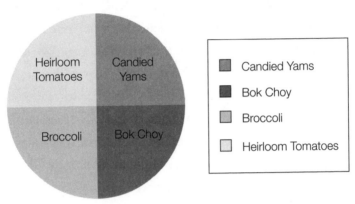

See how easy, fun, and informative this chart is to read? Simple lines and curves, a nice, inviting shape, and most importantly, instantaneous, relevant information you can trust.

As opposed to THIS squiggly line graph:

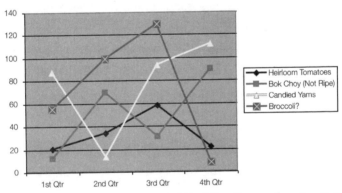

Fun? No. Easy? Not even close. Informative? You tell us. Sure, we know how to read this graph, but we can't expect you to be able to do so. And we sure as hell wouldn't trust this information when there's money on the line.

Our takeaway advice on the stock market? Don't overthink it! Trust your gut—you know a good company when you see it (e.g., Mercury Sable). Once you've made the investment, set it and forget it. Check back every few years to see how you're doing, but don't lose sleep over it. You've got a guy who screams on the floor of the stock exchange who you can trust (like ours with the answering machine), and that's the best you can hope for on this Great American Scream Machine we call Wall Street.

DOLLAR BILLS' TIP #129

When it comes to graphs and charts, place your trust in pie charts only—never the kind with squiggly lines.

Inheritance

There are those who say inheritance is not an investment strategy. They say it's ghoulish, disrespectful, and lazy to wait by the clock for a loved one to die. The Dollar Bills are sympathetic to the deceased—it must be terrible to be dead—but we're not in the business of weeping over the departed. We're in the business of making you money.

The first step is to identify a relative with money. This part is pretty easy. As soon as you are able to write as a child, start to keep inventory of who buys you which gifts around the holidays. The grandfather who buys you a fleet of motorized Big Wheels and season tickets to the Seattle Mariners is a hitter. The aunt who knits you a scarf isn't worth your time. Cut her off. As you get older, take notice of what kind of car everyone is driving and look at the labels of clothing worn by uncles whenever possible (Fubu dress shirts? Ding! Ding! Ding!). Although we do not officially endorse the practice, there are ways of "borrowing" logins and pin codes to double-check balances in checking and investment accounts. Surely a close relative wouldn't mind your checking up on his financial well-being. Once you have that information, it's time to mark your target. For the sake of argument, let's call him Uncle Pete.

First thing you want to do is to get a guys-only Vegas trip on the calendar. If he is who you think he is, Uncle Pete will pick up the tab for the room and the two of you will be bonding into the wee hours of the morning at a Pai Gow Poker table at Harrah's while the other relatives are passed out up in the suite. Maybe you get Uncle Pete a hooker in the "What happens in Vegas . . ." spirit, only to hold it as a bargaining chip later. Advantage: you. While you're at it, you may as well get a few hookers. You can get in on the fun, and more importantly, you'll be able to see the old guy in action, which will help you gauge how close he is to the finish line.

From there, build the relationship with biannual activities where you begin to squeeze out other, less deserving relatives. How does this photo album look to you? Hey, it's you and Uncle Pete hang-gliding the Grand Canyon! Hey, it's you and Uncle Pete kayaking the Amazon! And look at this one, you and Uncle Pete doing one-armed push-ups inside the Vatican on your month-long trip to Italy. The rest of the family will almost certainly wonder if you and Uncle Pete are gay for each other. That's fine. See if they still think you're gay when he leaves you his priceless collection of autographed *Playbill*s from Broadway shows spanning six decades. Who's gay now?

When Uncle Pete is on his deathbed, deliver a tear-filled speech, while he's still conscious, in case he's making any last-minute revisions to his final will and testament. You can just lift one from a movie; let's be honest, Pete's not going to know the difference. Recommendation: Hackman's locker room speech at the end of *Hoosiers*. That one gives everybody chills, even if they're about to die. If that fails, go right into Mel Gibson's epic in *Braveheart* where he's firing up those ragtag dudes to fight the dudes who had nicer outfits and horses. The message of Scottish freedom won't make total sense for the deathbed, but again, it won't really matter at that point. RIP, Uncle Pete.

Note: Do not attempt to kill Uncle Pete. This will completely undo all your work. You can't much enjoy the fruits of your labor if you're busy carving soap into a knife inside the walls of a state lockup. Hang in there—death often takes longer than we want it to. Uncle Pete will die. It's like Heinz Ketchup says—good things come to those who wait.

Your Credit, Your Debt

There's no greater investment one can make than an investment in personal debt. We'll stop and give you a moment to change your undershorts. Better now? Yeah, we just said out loud that running up debt is the best investment you can make. We'd shout it from a mountaintop if Richter didn't have these damn lower back problems that prevent him from doing as much hiking as he'd like to do. He's fine on even terrain, but you give him a pack and an incline and it really starts to flare up. But you're not worried about Richter's back trouble. You're worried about making shitloads of money.

Here's a pop quiz, hotshot (classic Dennis Leary line from *Speed*): If we gave you a small piece of plastic that fit conveniently into your fanny pack and that could be presented in place of paper money to purchase goods and services, would you accept? What if we also said you could just pay off a little of your bill every month for as long as you live? Oh, and what if we gave you ten different cards from different companies all under those same terms? Would you take that deal, hotshot? We don't like to cheat on quizzes, but the answer is: HELLZ YES!*

American Express, Visa, MasterCard, Discover, Diners Club, Blockbuster: Think of them as your tickets to the lifestyle you've always wanted but could never afford. It's like they say in the world of underground Go Fish tournaments: "If you ain't got the cards, you ain't got shit." The math is pretty simple on this, gang: The credit card companies require only that you pay a small percentage of your monthly bill. Weird business model, right? Let's say you purchase a new Rolls-Royce Phantom for $450,000 on your Discover card. The monthly minimum on that bill is something like $250 (need to double-check that, but it's in the ballpark). That's to say nothing of the fact that Discover is the card "that pays you back" (pretty sure that means they reimburse you for whatever you buy—brilliant marketing!). Bottom line? You just got a new Rolls-Royce with curtains in the back seat for literally nothing. They say our country is "addicted to plastic" like it's a bad thing. We'll take an addiction any day of the week to a plastic drug that gets us free luxury automobiles with curtains in the back so we can French-kiss skanks in privacy while we cruise down the Pacific Coast Highway.

We know this is a lot for the layman to digest so we've

---

*Note: Cheating is a critical part of business, but never admit to it out loud or in print.

boiled down our credit philosophy to what we call "The 5 Cs." They are: Cancun, convertibles, cognac, chinchilla coats, and cuticles. We burn up our plastic on long weekends in Cancun, imported drop-top automobiles, expensive aged *digestifs,* full-length real animal-skin coats, and biweekly manicures. Maybe you'd replace one or more of the "Cs" with a "C" of your own (cigarette boats, chopper rides inside volcanoes, or cigar store Indians for the den to name just a few), and that's the beauty of the credit card—your imagination is the limit. Now before you start barking about "bad credit" and "FICO scores," consider this: No one's gonna be asking about your FICO score (whatever that is) when you're power-chugging a yard glass full of strawberry-banana daiquiri from the porch of your three-bedroom timeshare condo overlooking the Señor Frog's in Cancun. Catch my drift, *señor?*

THE 5 Cs OF CREDIT

Cancun

Convertibles

Cognac

Chinchilla Coats

Cuticles

So, yes, you can get free cars and Mexican vacation homes (and trust us, that is all beautiful) but credit cards aren't just about all the awesome shit you can get on deep discount—they're about how you're perceived. As we've discussed many times in the pages of this important investment manual, and will continue to discuss until it sinks in, three-quarters of the battle of being rich is *looking* rich. That's why it's critical to get all your credit cards with platinum or "black" status. It's like having the highest level of clearance at the White House—either you're in the Oval Office or you're just another schmuck wearing a badge and giving tours. Platinum cards get you in the Oval Office of life.*

Let us paint a picture: You're out on a date with some smokin' hot twenty-three-year-old broad you met at the video arcade while posting the high score on Golden Tee (again). The check comes and you whip out a wallet glistening with platinum. Now, bear in mind, most of the cards will have been canceled by the credit companies because you haven't paid your bill in years (not your problem). You draw out the Delta SkyMiles Amex between your first two fingers and flick it out to the waiter without ever looking at him—you're too busy seducing the chick from the arcade. The waiter comes back with the card and tells you it's not working. That's when

---

*Without having to do all the presidential press conferences, stuffy dinners, and long, boring budget meetings.

you close the deal with this Golden Tee groupie by berating the waiter loudly and showing the girl what a real man looks like. Then give the guy another card (which you won't pay either). From there, Little Arcade Annie will melt in your hands like the molten chocolate that spilled from inside that cake you had for dessert. Looks like there'll be one more course to this meal.* A healthy roster of credit cards doesn't just get you luxury automobiles on the cheap, friends—it also gets you tons of Grade-A ass from local video arcades.

So that's Investing 101, Dollar Bills style. Bet you didn't learn any of that from your propaganda-spouting, tenured high school Econ teacher. You're ready now for that day at the zoo. If you're going to follow our aggressive investing tips, you'd better leave the kids at home—we're getting in the goddamn polar bear cage. Some of us (the pussies) are coming out in body bags. The rest of us are leaving in helicopters bound for the Hamptons. See you on the beach. We'll be the super-bronzed, ripped dudes playing Aerobie and pounding Bacardi Silvers. If you can't identify us by those clues, just look for the polar bear Speedos.

Oh, one last thing—we recognize that by purchasing this exclusive investment guide, you've paid a premium for the Dollar Bills brand. As a gesture of thanks, we'd like to offer a

*Fast, awkward, but still awesome intercourse is the "course" to which we are referring.

few of our tightly guarded personal investment strategies that have performed with varying degrees of success. We learned about giving the freebee from our weed dealer who always gives us a little extra from his personal stash when we buy in bulk. He calls it "takin' care of the regulars." So smoke up and enjoy!

SHHHHHHH!

The Dollar Bills Share Some of Their Top Secret Personal Investment Secrets

1. **Prince of Nigeria Foundation** (The Prince will typically e-mail you directly, to make it easy. Plus, African philanthropy looks good on the résumé.)

2. **Invest in China** (Especially the General Tso's chicken! Dee-lish!)

3. **Bribery/Extortion** (Take compromising photographs of prominent public figures.)

4. **Off-Track Betting** (Why go to the race when the race will come to you?!)

5. **Male Prostitution** (Nothing wrong with putting yourself on craigslist on occasion to make ends meet. Right, guys? Am I right? Guys?)

When meeting with someone for the first time, each time he/she begins to say something, start typing on your BlackBerry, or any kind of handheld device—even if you only have a cordless phone or calculator. It sends the message: I'm 30 to 35 percent interested in your answer to my question, because I'm so focused on emerging markets and early adoption of technologies.

Willie & Boyd's Notes:

We started by going to the Cincinnati Zoo (we were in town anyway for a Reds-Astros three-game series) to see if we had what it takes to wrestle the polar bears. Willie actually soiled his cargo shorts at the very sight of their exhibit, so we just hit the food court and went home.

Between us, we applied for and received 19 credit cards. We maxed out all of them, but were discouraged to find Rolls-Royce dealers do not take the Discover card as the Dollar Bills indicated they would. We've paid the minimum on every card for about a year now and we are living the Life of Riley! There are PT Cruisers in the driveway, full Rooms-to-Go living room sets in the house, and unlimited breadsticks from Domino's whenever the hell we feel like it. The creditors that used to harass us for not paying our bills have disappeared. Why? Because we use only disposable phones which we throw into Dumpsters after every call we make. Boyd loves to end his calls by saying "This is the Bourne Ultimatum!" and then hanging up. It's a hoot. Thanks for the tip, Dollar Bills!

We also dove into the real estate market using the Dollar Bills' unorthodox methods. The results have been mixed. We've been making huge offers on multimillion-dollar mansions and throwing away the terrorist phones before the Realtor can call us back on them. We feel a little silly saying this because we know there's always a strong financial theory driving everything the Dollar Bills do, but we can't seem to find the value in this particular technique. We thought we'd be known as the Donald Trumps of our community, but instead people just think we're the guys who make weird prank calls to local Realtors. I guess our biggest achievement has been stealing real estate signs from around town and putting them all in our buddy Carter's yard. Funny, but not super-lucrative.

And finally, Boyd went ahead and entered into an inappropriate relationship with his rich Uncle Reggie as the Dollar Bills suggested. It started as one too many beers at the American Legion hall on a weeknight and has escalated into weekend camping trips in a one-man pup tent. Let's just say, Boyd's spot in the will is locked!

Section 4

Your Business

Chapter Nine

The Billion-Dollar Idea

If our middle school French serves us, the word "entrepreneur" literally means "to enter and pretend." But what does the word mean, nonliterally and non-French? It means to be ahead of the curve. To buck convention in favor of mega-bucks. To *enter* into business agreements which basically give you the power to print money. To *pretend* that you don't really care about what happens to the economy, because you are blazing your own path. Every blaze starts with the spark of a great idea. If you want to start a forest fire, sometimes all you need is a lit cigarette and a pile of dry leaves. Here are some of the big ideas that started a five-alarm cash inferno for us. Let's see if it sparks some of your own.

Cristal Car Wash

This was our first jackpot. Several (fiscal) years ago, when we were just getting started in the business of success, we made a key realization: People will always pay a premium for goods and services that appear to be high-class or luxurious. Think about the examples of this you see every day: Five-star hotels, six day/five night cruises of the Great Lakes, front row seats to a Justin Guarini concert, and the window table at Macaroni Grill. It's no secret that people want to feel special.

Remember, wealth is 79 percent appearance, 19 percent hedge funds, and 8 percent mink parkas. As we consistently preach, this is a crucial state of mind. The appearance of prestige and luxury is precisely what drives people to pay more for things they associate with these qualities. People clamor for Guarini tickets because they give these people status among their peers—the tickets validate their lives (and who knows, maybe Kelly Clarkson will sit in for a couple duets!).

From an entrepreneurist perspective, nothing is more satisfying than identifying a weakness in people and exploiting it for your own gain. With this in mind, we conducted several hours of intense Google research to identify and home in on this cultural trend—willingness to pay extra for something

The Breakdown of Wealth

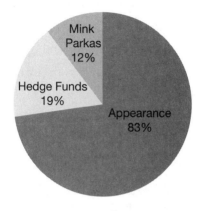

more expensive. We used this key market data to build the business model for our first* Cristal Champagne Car Wash.

The idea was exactly what it sounds like: create a high-end car wash that uses Cristal champagne ($400/bottle) instead of water. What could be more prestigious than watching top-shelf bubbly trickle down the sides of your Infiniti as paid Maxim models and handsome gents in formalwear massage the Cristal into the doors and hood. If you find yourself shouting "They're crazy!," trust us, you are not alone. For months we received nothing but rejection from every venture capitalist, bank, celebrity, doctor, lawyer, and relative

*And only, but first nonetheless.

we solicited. As you embark on your own entreprenurialistic journeys, it's during this phase when your true grit and moxie shine through. Most people quit when they get their first several dozen "get the fuck out of my office" responses. They will "enter" the arena, but won't "pretend" that they can make it. Let this fact soak in: You never actually make it until you pretend to make it. Only then can you proudly print the Entrepreneur business cards (preferably on heavy stock with lots of embossing and gold leaf).

Well, we ignored the *no's*, because those people didn't *know* what they were missing. And you *know* what? Eventually we landed the big fish, and secured substantial funding for our endeavor.* Were we taking a risk? You bet. Actually, not really since it was someone else's money, but there certainly was risk involved. Our market analysis had yielded a hypothesis and we proved it: Washing cars with super-expensive champagne brought with it a hefty overhead, sure, but the upside was astronomical. Surprise, surprise, we were right. Within six months, we had washed tens of cars.

We can admit now, without fear of prosecution, that we routinely rummaged through the cars to find loose change, sunglasses, and CDs we would sell to buy more Cristal and

*$7,245 less fees via a third mortgage against our houseboat.

fine suede rags. Whether or not people realized we were doing it is irrelevant. They were happy with the high sheen our wash and wax created. They were pleased with our 5-star service and they loved the fact that we wore formal tuxedos with tails while we cleaned their vehicles. It wasn't until months later that we learned of the damaging chemical reaction that occurs when champagne is sun-baked onto car paint, but by that point, we had moved on to the next venture.

Did we make millions and/or a profit on this business? Was the company investigated by the Better Business Bureau of Albuquerque, NM? Are we technically liable for the damage to the cars we washed? We may never know. All we can tell you is that with the right business plan, professional agility, and a winning smile, you can chart your own course. And a Cristal Car Wash is a VIP choice.

Kanda-Par

In the spring of 2003, President Bush (the younger one) enlisted the United States military (along with 40–50 soldiers from Trinidad and Tobago for backup) to lead a crucial, multinational mission into Iraq. Their objective was to find a bunch of secret nukes (WMD model) and kick the crap out of Saddam Hussein for trying to kill Bush's dad, President Bush (the older one). As far as we know, it all went as planned—

Bush (the younger one) got the nukes, tore Saddam a new one, and in the meantime, was able to officially deliver freedom, firmly establish democracy, and handily gain a public approval rating in Iraq of over 94 percent.*

While President Bush was tying up loose ends in Iraq, we turned our focus back to a war-ravaged country it seemed many American investors had forgotten: Afghanistan. We understood quickly what most people did not: There exists tremendous potential for businessmen who have the smarts, balls, and good looks to storm into Afghanistan and make things happen, just like Bush (the younger one) did when he rounded up all the terrorists and nukes in Iraq. Even almost a decade on now in the war in Afghanistan, the place is ripe for savvy entrepreneurs to strike while the iron is still hot and take advantage of the opportunity of a lifetime.

And, believe us, our government is taking notice. As you may or may not be aware (we weren't until just the other day), the United States military has basically taken up residence in Afghanistan. The goal, at least publicly, is to chase a bunch of Taliban terrorists with long, confusing names, but those of us "in the know"—really just the two of us at the moment—have a different theory: Maybe the government is actually just trying to follow our lead and get in on the game.

---

*It's our understanding that by the end of his term, his domestic numbers were even higher.

What's the game, you ask? Well, simply put, it's the gentleman's game. We've done extensive research on the region (we watched *Syriana*, *Mulan*, and *Bend It like Beckham* on Laser-Disc, all in one sitting last weekend) and we believe this society is ripe for Western modernization. Change, our research shows, should come in the form of upscale golf courses and private country clubs.

Imagine the Afghan people finally laying down their arms, taking up the peaceful game of golf, and embracing local heroes like Phil Mickleson, Retief Goosen, and Charles Howell III instead of Osama bin Laden and Omar Sharif. Now imagine yourself collecting greens fees and membership dues from the millions of Afghan natives who want to be like Goosen and the gang. Finally, imagine these golf courses being a place where Pashtuns, Kabuls, and Kardashians (the warring tribes in the region) can all come together in peace and prosperity, to celebrate the finer things in life—crushing steak, cabernet, and cigars in the Men's Grill.

This is a business plan that will not only generate enormous profit margins, but also enormous community value, and we're all about giving back to the community (not really, but it's good business to say stuff like that). Obviously you never want to sacrifice the former (money) to gain the latter (kiss-ass community credit), but if you can get both, all the better. Politicians and pundits alike will be too busy praising you for your vision and values to notice that you're collecting coin hand over fist.

True, executing the plan has its hurdles, but that will be the case for any great idea. First step is bulldozing a few hundred thousand acres of landmines. This could be potentially dangerous, so you'll want to spring for the extra insurance on the dozers when you're filling out the rental application. There's also the issue of reshaping the topography. The mountains will need to be leveled, and the dusty, arid ground will need to be converted into lush, rich soil. But that's what the day laborers are for. Head to any Home Depot parking lot and you can find several men ready to work for minimum wage. Get them on the first plane to Kandahar. They've got work to do.

It's important to note: You're going to want to put these steps into action *before* attempting to actually purchase the land. We know, this may seem risky to the novice entrepreneur, but think about it—you need to be certain that this is really the right spot for your courses, before you make the pricey land investment (not to mention all the goddamned sod and pro shop merchandise you'll need to buy).

Next is what we like to call **ancillary revenue**. Build lavish clubhouses with 5-star restaurants. Serve caviar, chilled lobster salad, and top sirloin fajitas with passion fruit chutney. Sell sweater vests, argyle socks, fuzzy clubhead covers, all with your corporate logo. Offer free guest passes to the sauna as prizes in a weekly business card drawing. By doing so, you'll get

This is the canvas.

With the right plan and roughly $79,000 down, this is the masterpiece.

people in the door, and can up-sell them on the comprehensive (and pricey) spa membership as they're enjoying the complimentary Aqua Velva, mouthwash, and disposable razors.

Plain English Guide to Confusing Financial Terms
Ancillary Revenue: Extra cash derived from an already brilliant idea. Like when you open a lucrative ice cream parlor and then sell drugs and bootleg movies out the back door for a little added cheese.

Finally, once all the pieces are in place, head out to the first tee and enjoy the spoils. Remember, watch out for the dogleg on 8, and avoid the beach on 13!

Other Billion-Dollar Ideas

$ **Timeshares.** Pick an exotic but underexposed location. **Hint:** The coast of Somalia has some deals right now on one- to two-bedroom condos. During the high season (TBD on specific dates), the rental fees alone will make your head spin.

$ **Domain Names.** "Content is king" as they say. Snatch up as many domain names as you can, and then just sit back and wait for the desperate buyers to come knocking. **Hint:** Keep your antennae up for major brand names. Just think how much you could get for ebay.com, nike.com, or google.com . . . and who knows, someone may fall asleep at the wheel and forget to renew on time. Always be ready to strike.

$ **Cloning. Hint:** If one Tiger Woods makes millions of dollars each year, how much do you think 50 Tiger Woodses would make?

$ **Movie Rights.** Secure the movie rights to people's lives, and make a killing. **Hint:** Your first goal should be finding Osama bin Laden. When you're finally able to track him down, convince him to sign over the movie rights to his life before you turn him in. Think about how much you could make selling that sucker to the networks as a Movie of the Week.

$ **Buy the Yankees.** Big price tag? Yes. But you've got to step up and make a move if you want to get ahead as an entrepreneur. **Hint:** If, for some reason, this deal falls apart, it's our understanding the Myrtle

Beach Pelicans are looking for minority investors. Not sure if that means you have to be a minority, but it's worth a look. Just get in the game.

$ **War.** Invest in building an army of contract killers, snipers, and jujitsu-trained mercenaries. Next, start a war with a small, shitty Third World country that you can basically overrun. **Hint:** Once you've taken control of the country, go to the U.N. for relief money. Trust us, they've got deep pockets and bleeding hearts.

DOLLAR BILLS TIP #79

Always throw your keys to a valet guy. Don't look at him, just throw your keys in his direction while saying something like: "Put her in the shade," "Keep her close," or "These rims cost more than you'll make this year." It lets people know you're top dog in the pecking order and an executive to be taken very seriously.

Willie & Boyd's Notes:

You may be thinking that these guys are completely out of their minds. Champagne car washes, golf courses in Kandahar, cloning Tiger Woods? Well, the light bulb probably sounded pretty darn crazy to Thomas Edison's buddies too. The Dollar Bills' entrepreneurial success stories inspired us, but proved difficult to execute. We burned through our venture capital on the first weekend of the Cristal Car Wash. That shit is really expensive. There were some hot high school cheerleaders controlling the marketplace with a sudsy $10 car wash right across the street. Ours cost $500. Hey, as the Bills say, "You're not gonna win 'em all, but all it takes is one."

That one also turned out not to be a golf course in Afghanistan. We're a little ashamed to admit that this one barely got off the ground for us. We rented a frontloader at the Kandahar John Deere dealership, but we came under heavy insurgent fire within minutes of dozing the proposed site of our 36-hole, Gary Player–designed course. We were held hostage for weeks before a team of American Green Berets rescued us in a daring mission. We feel like we failed, but again, we gave it a shot and that feels good.

One thing with a little more promise: We've taken the liberty of cashing out a fairly sizable portion of our wives' 401(k) accounts and investing in a small group of beachfront condos just south of Mogadishu. Pretty quiet on the rental front so far, but we're keeping our fingers crossed that things pick up over the 4th of July.

Chapter Ten

Small Business, Big Bucks!

Let's face it. As much as we all love the glitz and glamour of marquee, global brands like Nike, Microsoft, TWA, and Swatch, it's the small business owners who are the backbone and the heartbeat of this great nation. Some of the country's most iconic business figures began their careers running **mom-and-pop companies**, and small business owners continue to play a critical role in maintaining the health of our economy. They're like the Anthony Edwards of *ER*. Not as charming and charismatic as Clooney, not as adorable as Noah Wyle, but shit, someone's got to actually do the goddamn operations, right?? Unfortunately, despite their minuscule market shares, these small business owners shoulder the brunt of the load when things get tough. Apparently only Clooney and Wyle deserve to get a tan and do some snorkeling off the coast of Barbados, and have Uncle Sam pick up the bill.

Plain English Guide to Confusing Financial Terms
Mom-and-Pop Company: A company (Lachey Laser Tag is one of the most celebrated examples) that services lots of hot moms, and thus becomes a business with tons of pop, i.e., flashiness and/or Diet Fanta.

Over the past few years, we've seen huge, highly profitable corporations, like FEMA, AIG, and Brangelina, exposed as models of excess and inefficiency. Yet these companies are bailed out by the government when the shit hits the fan, having been deemed **too big to fail.** And who are we to disagree—a failure to release *Tomb Raider 2* and *Tomb Raider 3* would have catastrophic ramifications on our way of life— like in *Tomb Raider 1*, when society as we know it was on the verge of collapse. So yes, Brangelina and these other companies *are* too big to fail. However, as massive corporations are being pulled from the burning building we call the economy, small business owners all across the country are left to burn and perish, like Kurt Russell in *Backdraft*. They've essentially been deemed "too small to really give a shit about," and there's no bailout in sight. Many have been forced to shut their doors. Others continue to impishly endure the blazing inferno without having a clue as to how to fight back. It's pathetic, really.

Plain English Guide to Confusing Financial Terms
Too Big to Fail: When a Wall Street company is so awesome that it literally can't fail. Also the title of an upcoming Rocco Siffredi adult film.

Well, we're here to protect you, Mr. Small Business Owner, and to provide you with a huge hose and a sweet axe you can use to finally fight back. This chapter will serve up some tips on how you can beat the system, and take back your future, by thinking outside the box. Read on.

The following transcripts are taken from our internationally syndicated, critically lauded, oft-referenced, Internet-only investment show, ***DOLLAR BILLS***. Use this information to transform the way you approach your small business operations, and prepare yourself to reap the rewards of our hard work.

TRANSCRIPT—*DOLLAR BILLS*

Small Business, Big Bucks Segment: 401(k) Accounts and Traveler's Checks

RICHTER: Good evening, I'm Bill Richter.

LACHEY: And I'm Bill Lachey, and this is *Dollar Bills*. It's time to get down to business. Small business. This is a little segment we like to call "Small Business, Big Bucks!"

RICHTER: There are millions of small business owners out there listening to this show right now, and we're talking directly to you. Think of us as your co-workers, right there in the break room with you, splitting a croissant and some French vanilla coffee.

LACHEY: Make mine a Grande! Hey! Who used the last of the creamer?! (*chuckling*) Okay, so how, as a small business owner, do you take the next step toward the big bucks? We've got some tips today that will inject your limp little business with some much needed testoster-logic, as we like to call it, and change your bottom line forever.

RICHTER: You said it, Bill. Number one, and I *cannot stress this enough, people*—Hire, hire, hire. It's as important to a small business owner as "location, location, location" is to a restaurant owner, real estate developer, or chauffeur.

LACHEY: I.e., *very* important . . . and here's why. Each person you bring on, full-time with benefits, means an additional 401(k) plan for you to match, dollar for dollar. This allows you to basically dump money into the stock market.

RICHTER: Why is this a good move? Think about it! Because when a couple months go by, and you fire them for insubordination, guess what? That money has grown tenfold, compounded with interest, FICA/FICO, and capital gains. You gotta stay on target here, people!

LACHEY: As the losers are reading their pink slips, you collect the untouched revenues. You see, the rule here, people, is that individuals can't tap these 401(k) accounts until they *retire*. Well, what if they don't ever have a chance to retire, because you can the shit out of them?

Stay on Target with 401(k)

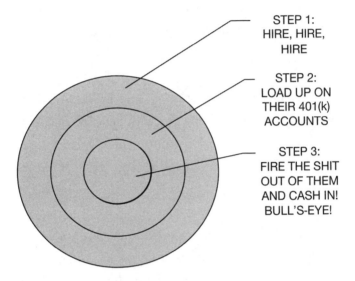

STEP 1:
HIRE, HIRE,
HIRE

STEP 2:
LOAD UP ON
THEIR 401(k)
ACCOUNTS

STEP 3:
FIRE THE SHIT
OUT OF THEM
AND CASH IN!
BULL'S-EYE!

RICHTER: Case closed! The money, plus interest, is back in your account before they've hit the parking lot. Whooo!

LACHEY: So that's point one. Point B is even more simple. From this moment forward, you should be paying for all your business expenses—and personal expenses—in traveler's checks.

RICHTER: (*facetiously*) But Bill . . . I'm confused . . .

(*intense*) Wake up here people! It's called "tax credits."

LACHEY: Let me lay this out for you viewers at home. There's a reason they're called *traveler's* checks. See, when you pay for business expenses with traveler's checks, there is no way on God's green earth the government, not to mention the IRS, can verify where your company is actually based.

RICHTER: So let's say Pat Sandles in Wichita has a sandals store, "Pat's Sandles," where he sells men's sandals and braided belts. Pat also knows that Kansas has the highest tax rate in the country for small businesses.

LACHEY: Way to go, Pat!

RICHTER: So what does Pat do? He collects money from his sandals and braided belt sales and immediately marches down to the local bank to convert that money into traveler's checks.

LACHEY: That way, when he has to pay his rent, his heating bill, he has to buy more of those silver foot size machines, mannequin feet, or some hooks to hang the belts in his store, he does not get taxed on those expenses. Let me repeat that: *He does not get taxed on those expenses.*

RICHTER: Trust me . . . the Kansas government is way too busy dealing with tort reform and pitching the 2020 Olympics to occupy themselves with trying to unravel this freakin' mystery.

LACHEY: It's 100 percent legit, and 110 percent good business.

RICHTER: Tune in next week for more small business strategies, and until then, remember . . .

UNISON: Know your business, don't let your business know you!

THINKING OUTSIDE THE BOX

No matter who you are, sometimes in life, you hit a slump. Just like a major league slugger, as a small business owner, you occasionally hit a tough streak where you just can't quite see the ball. Don't be discouraged when this happens. It's your mind telling you to step out of the batter's box for a second and think. This is where the classic saying originated.

You've got to *think outside the box*. Let your rational self and your inner artist self make sweet love to one another. Not the over-the-clothes-petting type of intimacy the rigid "industry experts" would suggest. We're talking about really letting it fly. Some seriously hard-core shit. Like one-of-the-hookers-might-dislocate-her-shoulder type of relations. This kind of raw, personal carnal knowledge is essential for you to fully access your mojo as a small business owner, and blast that hanging curveball straight out of Madison Square Garden.

Read the following transcript to learn about a businessman, Frank Bishop, who is in need of some out-of-the-box thinking to bust open his faulty business plan and refashion it a winner.

TRANSCRIPT—*DOLLAR BILLS*

Small Business, Big Bucks Segment: B&E Incorporated

LACHEY: Welcome to *Dollar Bills,* I'm Bill Lachey.

RICHTER: And I'm Bill Richter. We've got a great show today, so let's get it on. This is a segment we like to call "Small Business, Big Bucks!"

LACHEY: That's right Bill. Today, we're going to talk to a small business owner who's looking for advice on how to grow his fledgling company. Say hello to Frank Bishop, the founder and CEO of Bishop Home Security. Frank, thanks for joining us today.

RICHTER: Frank.

FRANK BISHOP: Gentlemen, a pleasure to be here.

RICHTER: So Frank, Bill and I are eager to help you improve your game plan. Why don't you start by telling us a little bit about your company, Bishop Home Security.

FRANK BISHOP: Thanks Bill and Bill. Bishop Home Security provides homeowners with state-of-the-art home security systems, including burglar alarms, carbon monoxide detectors, and smoke detectors. Our real purpose is to provide people with peace of mind. I started the company in 1999 with 3 employees, and now I've got a staff of over 50, operating in and around Santa Fe.

LACHEY: (*thinking, staring off into space*) Uh huh . . .

RICHTER: And how have you been able to stand out in the marketplace, and keep the company on the rise?

FRANK BISHOP: Well, we really focus on customer service, reliability, and—

LACHEY: (*light bulb goes off*) Uh oh, Richter: I think I just stepped outside the box.

RICHTER: Heyo! Mind if I join you, Lachey?

LACHEY: Indeed, good sir. Okay—consider the stats: We know that over 95 percent of Americans have been the victims of a B&E within the last five years, right? Even our houseboat got hit last year.

FRANK BISHOP: Those stats are not—

RICHTER: That's a great point, Bill. People these days are desperate to dump money into their homes to foil the burglars, scam artists, and animal rapists who would take advantage of their leaving town.

FRANK BISHOP: Gentlemen, if I may—

RICHTER: You *may* sit back quietly, Frank, and watch genius in action. We're about to revolutionize the home security industry.

LACHEY: There's always been a lot of money to be made on fear of home invasion, but it's time for some fresh thinking to be injected into the marketplace. Frank, instead of relying on these fancy machines that don't do a whole hell of a lot to protect Grandma's silverware, why not take control of the process? What if you guaranteed your clients that only *one* person would rob their homes while they're out of town.

RICHTER: Stay with us here, Frank. One of your employees busts into the place while Mr. and Mrs. Johnson are in the Adirondacks for the weekend and steals a predetermined list of items from the home, agreed upon by the Johnsons.

LACHEY: It takes the guesswork out of home security, Frank. Instead of wondering whether some creep is gonna clean them out completely, they can rekindle their romance with the peace of mind that they know exactly who's breaking in and exactly what will be taken while they're gone.

FRANK BISHOP: Are you . . . suggesting that I orchestrate a break-in?

LACHEY: I'm suggesting that you start thinking outside the box, Frank. You're not hurting these people. You're providing them with an insurance policy. You're providing them with *real* peace of mind.

RICHTER: Here's your new slogan, Frank, "Go with Bishop, or roll the dice and risk all your worldly possessions." King to rook 4, checkmate!! That's a chess reference, Frank. Boom!

LACHEY: Frank, it's simple. Offer people a sliding scale of services. For just $300, your "Associate Level" program provides a client with a licensed burglar who will come to their home, kick in a couple windows, shred their couch pillows, and steal their TV.

RICHTER: Right, right . . . Pony up a grand and reach the "Friend Level" where your certified staff will pick their locks, turn the house over, but only take a few of their DVDs and small toiletries.

LACHEY: I couldn't have said it better.

FRANK BISHOP: What? You can't be serious. I'm not even sure I get this.

RICHTER: Bill, this is pure gold. Especially in today's market, people can't be worrying about all their valuables falling into the wrong hands. Frank, you'll assure them that by giving up a little, they save a lot.

LACHEY: Something we preach every day. And here's another benefit: You'll give all the stolen items to charity, so not only do people feel safe, they also get to give back to the community. Translation: a pretty sweet tax break on the donation.

RICHTER: Which is reason enough right there. Frank, go build your new company. You're welcome.

Frank is a perfect example of someone who hit a slump with his small business, and needs to find a creative way to adapt to a marketplace that changes by the day. Even *we* have hit a couple slumps over the years (a mime-only talent agency and a "Legends of Serial Killing" line of action figures come to mind immediately). Fortunately for Frank, he was able to turn to us and get the answers he needed. We showed Frank how to take a step out of the batter's box, realign his perspective, step back in, and crush the next pitch off the scoreboard like Roy Hobbs in *The Naturalist*. Take these principles and apply them to your own small business. Remember, sometimes you need to take a moment and *think outside the box*. You'll be surprised at what happens next.*

*So will we. We honestly have no idea what happens next.

DOLLAR BILLS TIP #81

"Listening" goes a long way when negotiating a deal for your small business, but not as far as yelling.

Willie & Boyd's Notes:

As we've made our way through this guide, we've tried to overcome our skepticism about the Dollar Bills' principles for success, and to demonstrate to them that we're close to being ready to fly on our own. That has been really hard at times. For example, with that crackpot idea about starting a home security company and robbing people as an insurance policy. It's not just a terrible business concept, it's downright illegal. The Bills are always telling us not to "live by the laws imposed by some minimum-wage bureaucrat in Washington State," but this was one where we should have trusted our gut. Our case is still working its way through the courts.

The Bills always say though, "Losers complain. Hitters control the elements." We want to be hitters, so we're keeping the faith. Just a few weeks ago, we converted all of our liquid funds to traveler's checks, allowing us to spend without fear of taxation, or any form of recourse by the government. So far so good on that front. Brightly colored money that you get back if you "lose" it? Why didn't someone tells us about this sooner? Rest assured we "lost" a lot of money at dog tracks up and down the west coast of Florida. But no worry, we called Amex and got it all back. Great tip, Dollar Bills!

Chapter Eleven

A, B, CEO:

How to Nail the Interview and Land a CEO Job

CEO
Pronunciation: \,sē-(,)&ē-ˈō\
Function: noun
Etymology: Chief Executive Officer

Definition: The highest-ranking executive, with the chief decision-making authority in an organization or business.

Let's assume, for argument sake, that the entrepreneurial life, as illustrated earlier, is just not for you. You're a guy who feels more at home within the constructs of a conventional corporation. You generally prefer a safe bet to risking it all for a potentially monumental payoff. If you were cast in a movie, you'd play the nice guy, who is a really good friend to the hot chick, who lets her cry on your shoulder, who is there for her when she's dumped by our character. (We play the cool guy who's banging the hot chick and then dumps her for some even hotter chick after he kills all the bad guys.) Simply put, you're a company man. Well, we're pleased to say, there's still hope. Just because you're a company man, doesn't mean you can't be *the* company man.

You may have guessed by the title, and the above definition, that this chapter has something to do with becoming a CEO. This definition was pulled by our secretary from mysterious sources on the Internet,* and look, we'll be totally honest with you, we have no idea what fancy literary terms like "Etymology," "Function," or "Noun" mean, nor do we have the faintest idea what the holy hell that gibberish is next to "Pronunciation." Some kind of Egyptian Pharaoh tomb script, or computer hacking code, probably. So who can be sure of the true origins of this term and the associated information? But what we do know for certain is that the definition itself is real, and that it's the only one that matters.

In layman's terms, the CEO is the big dog. The decision maker. The shit runner. The man of the hour, 24 hours a day. CEOs are, of course, the favorite sons of American business.

---

*We initially requested that she retrieve it for us from the big, dusty books that line the dark oak shelves in the smoking lounge of our members-only men's club. Then we remembered that there are no chicks allowed.

Celebrated and honored in times of prosperity, compensated in times of hardship. Trusted with the keys to the kingdom, and armed with the powers of a king.* This is the job every single American dreams of, and only the most elite few ever experience.

So the question is, how does one become a CEO? Two ways seem apparent, though only one is worth pursuing. The first, and ill-advised, route, is to spend the majority of your adult life working your way up the food chain, from the mail room to the corner office. This is the route most Americans choose, and in the end, all they'll find is disappointment, in the form of twenty-five extra pounds, high blood pressure, and a yes-man mentality that will keep them below the glass ceiling in every aspect of their lives.

The second, recommended course of action is to go straight to the source, and interview solely for CEO jobs. That's where we come in. And while we haven't had to actually interview for anything in years (other than for cover stories for *Cigar Aficionado, GQ, Forbes*, and/or similar publications**), we're pretty sure we're still experts in impressing the pants off of conservative, hot, office manager chicks and/or dudes. Far too frequently, even when people have the right intention, they miss

*Definitely includes making demands for velvet, gold items, horses, and harlots. Not certain about the ability to call for public hangings.

**Mainly (entirely) for similar publications, specifically several blog entries on our Internet site.

out on great opportunities because they are either ill prepared, lack the confidence to **ask for the order,** or simply just don't understand the intricacies of executive-level deal making. The information that follows will serve as your handbook for navigating those very intricacies, nailing the interview, and landing that prized, cushy CEO gig.

What's that, Mr. Interviewer? The job opening is a temp data-entry position for minimum wage? Not anymore. You douchebags just found your new leader.

Plain English Guide to Confusing Financial Terms
Ask for the Order: Used frequently in high-stakes negotiations. Typically has one of two meanings: 1) Make your demands and close the deal, or, in some cases, 2) Order the surf-and-turf, or another pricey entrée, if the negotiations are taking place over lunch and said lunch is being paid for by your opponent.

Here we are, having just "asked for the order"—in this case, we're demolishing some endangered California freshwater jumbo shrimp—while the client stepped away to the restroom. He paid for it.

Look the Part

If you're going to convince the interviewers that you're the man for the job, you've got to look the part. And that means looking like you've been there before. "There" being the top. And "before" meaning that you've led several Fortune 500 companies to increased profitability/bankruptcy over the past decade. In other words, this is old hat for someone of your caliber.

First, dress for success. We recommend a custom-tailored double-breasted suit with a medium break on the pants. Richter prefers a double Windsor knot on the tie, which, incidentally, should be red. Why? Because red sends the message that you're out for blood. Not literally, though it probably doesn't hurt to allude to the fact that you've been in your fair share of bar fights. This lets them know you're: a) not going to take shit from anyone, b) still able to take care of business after a few Jäger bombs, and c) not afraid to make rash decisions.

Lachey also owns the room with his wardrobe, employing a leisurely yet sophisticated look to get his point across. And that point is: "I certainly don't need this job, because I'm already buried in coin and trim, and have a lot of sailing/golf/ fox hunting to do, but this place is so f—d up, it might be a fun challenge for a few months (but no Fridays)." In place of the crisp Oxford and power tie combo, Lachey typically opts for the classic silk-poly blend turtleneck, or a pastel golf shirt (collar up, always), under a custom-tailored blazer with gold-plated, monogrammed buttons. Regardless of your style (but it should be one of these two options if you want to get the job), dressing for success is the first step in becoming the CEO you've always dreamed of being.

Next up is making your entrance. This is every bit as important as your wardrobe in terms of establishing the right image. Pull up to the front of the building, hop out of your car,* and throw your keys at the nearest passerby, saying

---

*We recommend renting either a limousine or an exotic sports car, like a LeBaron convertible or Dodge Viper, if this is not what you are normally able to drive. Even if you have to drive the limo yourself, it still says "I'm accustomed to class and power."

"Keep her up front," as you stride past him or her, through the revolving lobby door. (Always carry a second set of keys, just in case.) In the event that there is no one out front when you arrive, or that you are escorted back out of the lobby by building security, don't fret. Always have a backup plan. Simply get back into your car, and park it in a reserved spot—preferably the existing CEO spot. This shows the company that you're familiar with the privileges that come with the gig, and you expect to receive them immediately. Image preserved.

Really want to turn some heads? Roll in old-school style, in a luxury leather- and velvet-adorned carriage. People will be absolutely blown away by your classiness and prestige. Plus, if, for some strange reason you don't get the job, maybe your prize steed will have dropped a monster deuce in the office parking lot.

Remember, HAVE FUN. The more people at the company see you having fun, the more they'll assume you're already rich as shit, like we are. You know who else is rich as shit? CEOs. You following this?

Once you're inside, and the interview begins, it's time to break out your microcassette Dictaphone. Understand this, and embrace it: CEOs never write or type anything themselves. Allow the interviewer to begin speaking, and then interrupt him/her by putting a hand up, and pulling the Dictaphone from your double-breasted suit pocket. Give a strong look of confidence when you place the Dictaphone on the table between you, and hit "record." Let the interviewer know that you'll be having one of your girls at the office transcribe your notes later that day.

It is always recommended that you bring two extra microcassettes ("extra tape stock") with you, in case the interview runs long, and/or the primary microcassette malfunctions and the tape becomes unwound all over the table. In addition to the extra tape stock, carry a small pencil with you, to deal with this second possibility. Calmly use it to rewind the tape while suggesting, in no uncertain terms, that you're going to need to take this up with your secretary when you get back to the office. This deflecting of blame is something CEOs should be well versed in. It will also serve to take the focus away from the mess you've created.

Set the Tone

So you've made your entrance. You look sharp as nails, your Dictaphone is cued up, and your tricked-out ride with tints and spoiler is out front getting a wash and wax (you wisely told the car wash guy to just charge it to the current CEO). Now you've got to set the tone of the meeting—to make it yours. You see, people have a tendency to be so thankful for the opportunity to interview for a job, and anxious to impress, that they allow the other person to control the meeting, from start to finish. You know where this gets you? A nice little nine to five position, two weeks vacation, and a certificate of appreciation on your 10-year anniversary, that's where. If you want to get serious about landing the big fish, you've got to manipulate your rod like you mean it. When it jerks, jerk it back. Set the hook, and steer the fish where you want it to go, with an intuitive grasp of the rod with one hand and a gentle, exploratory cradling of the reel with the other. Got it? So, how do you set the tone?

One of the most fail-safe ways to win over a stiff interview room is to enter bearing gifts. Your goal here is to immediately show these people you'll be a generous boss, so don't skimp. Perfume, monogrammed towels, a bunny rabbit, or a handmade gift certificate for a massage, from you, will not only put the interviewer at ease, but also provide a great distraction technique in the event you get in a jam. For instance, let's say the interviewer asks you a tough question you have no idea how to answer. Simply get on the ground and feed the rabbit some carrot shavings you've pulled from your pocket (you'll want to use a different pocket than the one for your Dictaphone). She'll almost instantly forget about wanting to know how you'll diversify domestic operations, and will instead be mesmerized by your love of animals. By the time you've returned to your chair, cradling the bunny, she'll be more likely to ask for your phone number than bother you with more corporate minutiae.

This little guy will not only help you through a tough spot in the interview, but may also get you some additional "perks," if you know what we mean . . . (nonmissionary sex with the interviewer is what we mean).

Once you've wowed the room with your lavish gifts, your next move should be to compliment the interviewer on her legs. Women love this shit. If it's a dude, tell him it looks like he can squat a shitload. Trust us, they will absolutely eat this up, and subsequently let down their guard. People want to know they'll be working for someone who appreciates them on a variety of levels, not just because they're good at Excel, or willing to work long hours. "But what about sexual harassment," you whine? Don't overthink, don't hesitate, and don't be a pussy. The only people who still get busted for sexual harassment these days are the guys who organize your run-of-the-mill, dudes-only tickle fights at their 50th birthday parties. Remember, you're giving them a compliment. Project power and entitlement, rather than creepiness. Do it right, and they'll thank you—with a job offer.

Act like a CEO

This may be the most important facet of a successful CEO interview campaign. You can look great, turn heads with lavish gifts, but if you don't act like a CEO, they'll never believe you've got what it takes to lead them to the promised land.

First and foremost, be aggressive. Companies want to know their CEO is going to kick ass first and ask questions later. So no matter what else you do, come in hot. Spin the chair around before you sit down with it facing backwards, so they know you're unconventional—you're a whiz kid who plays by his own rules and just might invent the next big Internet site, or the Internet itself. Or, if you want to project a more old-school image, kick your feet up on the table or desk. Relax. Clasp your hands behind your head, and start with something like "Okay, so where are we with the Johnson portfolio?" When they look at you quizzically, let them know you were just testing them, and that it's okay for them to ask the first question.

In each of these scenarios, you're convincingly playing the part of the CEO, and the more committed to the role you are, the more they will buy into what you're selling. Here's another surefire move: Don't be afraid to light up a smoke during the interview. Have you seen *Mad Men* lately?—those guys use cigarettes and Scotch to close deals, both in the boardroom and in the bedroom. While smoking is very likely to be against corporate policy nowadays (thanks a lot, liberals!), it shows the interviewer you're not afraid to take risks and challenge authority. The moment you fire up that Winston, you've made it very clear that you're not in the business of taking orders. You give them. There's a reason why this company is in search of a CEO (even if it's not): The current system just isn't working. It's time to shake things up a bit. Better yet, light up two Winstons simultaneously (like they do in all those classic war movies, like *Battlefield Earth* or *Pearl Harbor*) and give the interviewer one while staring intensely at her eyes and/or cans. Cans first, then eyes. Then, back to cans.

Whatever you do, do not prep. I repeat: Other than memorizing the information in this chapter, do not, under any circumstances, prep for this interview. The last thing you want is to come across as "knowing too much about the company"— that's the fastest way to appear overeager, and underqualified. Most importantly, that information simply doesn't matter. Landing the elusive CEO job is not about your subpar skill set, lack of meaningful business experience beyond entry-level positions, nor the utter confusion and heat flashes you feel when you read the corporate mission statement and by-laws. Your Hollywood leading man charisma, brash leadership style, and unbridled bravado will improve *any* organization, regardless of what it does. Peek behind the curtain for a moment, and you'll find that most CEOs don't have the first clue what their companies actually do. It's precisely this that makes them so powerful. They just don't give a shit. Being a CEO is about ripping power lunches, taking the Gulfstream V to London, Asia, or Europe for movie premieres, delivering keynote speeches, and signing mega-bonus checks to yourself. The sooner you realize and accept this, the sooner you'll be truly able to act like a CEO.

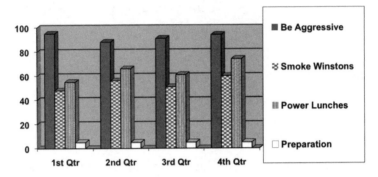

Talk like a CEO

A key component of selling yourself as the leader of the company is projecting a strong image of a progressive corporate strategist. To do this, pepper your answers and general conversation with corporate buzzwords. This will show them that you are a visionary, possessing a far more comprehensive understanding of the business than they do. Talk about the need for "rightsizing" the business and "pushing the envelope" to "drill down" on the company's "core competencies" and return the organization to "best of breed" with all the right elements "baked in" so it will be a "streamlined," "sustainable" model for success. You should literally make the quotations symbols with your fingers as you say each of these terms. It doesn't matter that you don't know what they mean. Frankly, we don't either. What matters is the message you're sending: You're aware that *they* have no idea what these words mean. Chuck a few "social media" references in there whenever possible, and let the interviewer know that while you'd love to visit with him/her all day, you have a "hard stop" at noon for an "offline" discussion with an investor you're "shepherding" through an **IPO**. But if there are any other thoughts or questions, they can ping you anytime.

Plain English Guide to Confusing Financial Terms
IPO: Investment Plan Overload. In a fast-moving market, novice investors often plan too much, and miss the boat. These people need handholding and shepherding.

Compensation and Perks

When the time comes to get down to business and talk specifics, the very first thing you should do is demand to know what the incentive package is. All the top execs have them. This sends a very clear message that you're not into wasting your time, or theirs. Yes, you're sure the base salary is very handsome and in the tens of millions, but what are the freakin' perks?! Included in your list of expectations should be a company car (preferably foreign, e.g., Datsun or Peugeot), six to eight weeks vacation, Clippers season tickets, access to the company houses in Reno, Branson, MO, and Ocean City, NJ, and the private cell numbers for Jessica Biel, Scottie Pippen, and Burt Reynolds. You should also be ready to take the discussion one step further, if you see an opening, to cover things like a private plane for your friends to use (in addition to yours), fur coats and hats, a tanning bed, and most importantly, a full set of major organs on reserve in the event you ever need one.

Other Key Perks

$ Viagra (shitloads of it, but on a "hush-hush" basis).

$ Star on the Hollywood Walk of Fame (this one may take a while, but don't relent . . . you're worth it).

$ Six-person Jacuzzi in your office, in the shape of a Lamborghini.

$ Personal Tae Bo instructor on call 24 hours a day.

$ Recording contract with a three-album guarantee.

Next, ask what your T&E budget is. You're being facetious, of course. You assume there is no budget limit for the CEO. And do they check details on the receipts? Because some may pertain to highly sensitive, confidential business (e.g., the all-day meeting and Gentleman's Special prime rib dinner at Jumbo's Clown Room). If they start to question you in more detail, make strong eye contact and calmly tell them, "In the current economy, you'll need to be able to leverage all of the company's paradigms and meet fiscal and/or EBITA projections, pre-tax dollars, obviously." They'll have no idea what you're talking about, because they're middle management, and are on a need-to-know basis.

Finally, what's your exit package? Tell them specifically that you want to receive an enormous bonus for breaking your contract early.

Negotiate to Win

When the time comes for the hard negotiation, put on your poker face and get down to business. Be prepared, and don't budge an inch (literally or figuratively), because their only goal will be to **ice you** and get you to sign on the dotted line for much less than you're worth.

Plain English Guide to Confusing Financial Terms
Ice You: Slang for "Isolate you," i.e., lock you in a musty, cramped room until you submit to certain demands, like a performance-based bonus, or a limit on your cell minutes.

Here are a couple tricks that will help you throw them off balance, take the upper hand, and blow this thing wide open, i.e., hit a freakin' home run, i.e., bag this thing, i.e., get the job.

- When they ask to see your résumé, tell them instead that you've prepared a more relevant document. Then slide a piece of paper over to them, on which you've written a very large number (in the high millions). As you slide it over, say, "This is all you need to review."
- During the negotiations, refer to the interviewer by a name that is close, but not exact. For example, if the interviewer's name is Dan, go with Stan. Bart for Mark, Doug for Jim, Cornelius for Steve, etc. While it's true that people generally like to have their names remembered, in this case it shows the interviewer that, as CEO, you may often have bigger fish to fry than dicking around with remembering everyone's specific information. You'll find that this sends a message of power, and power is every CEO's greatest weapon (unless you're the CEO of a weapons company).

Wrap It Up

When you win the negotiation and are hired on the spot, immediately fire the interviewer for challenging your authority. The employees must know that you run a zero tolerance operation, and from this point forward, should keep their heads down and do their fucking jobs, so you don't have to do yours (at least not the boring business/work parts). Good luck out there!

DOLLAR BILLS Tip #103

Invest in an enormous, ornate, ivory and marble fountain for your driveway. So big that you can barely maneuver your car around it. Each morning, have it filled with fresh bottled water and stocked with new Japanese fighting fish.

Willie and Boyd's Notes:

Ever since reading this chapter, we've been reevaluating the things we do in our respective office environments. All these years we've been climbing the ladder, when we should have taken the elevator to the top floor right from the beginning.

Admittedly, neither of us has yet taken the initiative to march up to our bosses and demand to interview for the CEO gig (in part because Dictaphones are pretty hard to find these days, and we want to be 100 percent prepared), but we have given a lot of thought to how we are perceived in the workplace. We hate to sound like a broken record, but the Dollar Bills were right again. We started with the small stuff: sitting with our chairs backwards, complimenting female co-workers on their tight bodies and their red-hot "whore heels," and chain-smoking, *Mad Men*-style, around the office. Guess what? Our colleagues are looking at us completely differently. Especially the ones in Human Resources. They seem especially impressed. If we'd known all it takes to get respect at work is a couple smacks on the ass and a few puffs on a Winston, we would have CEOs a long time ago. Where have you been all our lives, Dollar Bills?!

PS—We're going rabbit shopping this weekend. Stay tuned.

Section 5

Your Safety

Chapter Twelve

Security

In this Internet Age of interconnectivity with BlackBerrys, iPads, fax machines, and car phones, information travels at the speed of light. There is no speed limit on the Information Superhighway. Obviously we'd love that to be the case on the 405. We'd get a lot fewer tickets. But seriously, with data flying by like a Miata on the Autobahn, it's important to protect yourself from predators trying to intercept your personal information.

Did you know that more than four million people have their identities stolen every day? And not in the cool way, like when Nicholas Cage stole Travolta's identity in *Face/Off*. Well, just as that is one of the greatest movies of our time, identity hijacking has become one of the greatest problems we now face as a cyber society. (When speaking about technology, it's a good idea to use the word **cyber** as much as possible.) So, the question is, how do you keep your personal data safe? How do you make sure your Social Security number, your PIN, and your iTunes password don't fall into the wrong hands?

Plain English Guide to Confusing Financial Terms
Cyber: Awesome word that makes anything sound cutting-edge, like "I'm chillin' at a cyber-café," or "check out these new cyber-pants," or "I'm gonna catch a quick cyber-nap." Also a kickass martial arts film starring Jean-Claude Van Damme (the Muscles from Brussels).

Some credit card companies suggest it's as simple as changing your password every couple of months. Who has the time for that? Other so-called "experts" want you to shred your records. Oh, sure, let me just run over to my fancy document shredder and take care of that right away. For the record, we strongly recommend against investing in these machines. They take up space and look tacky in your home business center. Plus, the more you rely on them, the more powerful they become. Eventually, if we're not careful, we may reach a point where there's no way to tell who's controlling who. Do you want to reach that point?

Tacky. Low capacity. And may eventually lead to . . .

. . . THIS.

Are you ready to accept responsibility for THIS? I think you already know the answer to that question.*

*Photo courtesey of Takanishi Lab., Waseda University.

We're not advising you to keep sensitive (or incriminating) materials lying around. Heavens no. Quite the opposite. We get rid of our private Dollar Bills documents religiously, but frankly, most regular people get skittish when they have to "break into a private office complex" and "start a loosely controlled Dumpster fire." Nor can most people afford that much lighter fluid on a quarterly basis. But the fact remains, if your private information is left unprotected, *you* are unprotected. Just like Paul McCartney, when he got divorced from Yoko Ono, and she took him to the cleaners for millions.*

The bottom line is that serious threats require serious deterrents. Our solution is simple, user-friendly, and environmentally conscious**: Hire a body double and travel in a motorcade. Think anybody's stealing Obama's Netflix login information? Nope. Because he rides in a black Suburban with tinted windows. Do you think hackers are accessing the Pope's Hotmail account? Please. And we'll bet the farm that no one's using Kim Jong-il's Diners Club card without authorization. Why? Because all these people know the importance of protecting their assets in the Digital Age. And they do it with body doubles and bodyguards.

*Literally. When they got divorced, part of the settlement was a huge bill at the dry cleaners.

**Use the phrase "environmentally conscious" frequently, regardless of whether it has anything to do with what you're talking about. You'll find that people perk up to what you're saying.

Cyber thieves think twice when they see those guys wearing dark suits, shades, and those phone cords in their ears. Have your team flanking you when you surf the Web at home, or an Internet café. Roll up hot to the mall in your motorcade, hop out, and stride confidently amidst your guys as you window-shop, particularly when you pass or enter a technology store like Radio Shack, Best Buy, or IBM. People will see you as a man who has left nothing to chance, a man with protection greater than any **firewall** could ever provide. And the cyber hackers will be forced to look elsewhere to do their damage.

Plain English Guide to Confusing Financial Terms
Firewall: In the early days of the Internet, companies like Apple and Microsoft literally built huge walls around their offices and set them on fire, so that spies and intruders would be kept at bay. This technique, while effective, did not translate to the general consumer. Now, firewalls are installed, on a much smaller scale, within the actual computer. This is precisely why your laptop gets hot if you use it for a long time.

And if an entire security detail doesn't mesh with your family budget, you can just hire one of those big beefy guys in a tight black shirt, like Lindsay Lohan has following her around all the time. Ideally, you'll want this guy to be on the clock 24/7—Internet thieves never sleep, even though you do—but again, if you're dealing with budgetary constraints, at a bare minimum, he should accompany you at all times in public. This will project an image of security, even if the moment you get inside your house he heads upstairs to relax in a bubble bath or to watch old episodes of *$25,000 Pyramid*. By being seen out in public with this type of protection, you're letting the bad guys know that, this time, crime will NOT pay.

All it takes are the 3 Bs: Black Suburbans, Body Doubles, and Big Beefy Guys (in tight black shirts). Don't be a victim. It makes you sound like a pussy.

DOLLAR BILLS TIP #55

Start requesting that your friends and colleagues refer to you as "Our Dear Leader." It works for Kim Jong-il, and she seems to have it pretty freakin' easy, no? Once people get into the habit of calling you by your new name, you can shift your focus to shooting a 38 under par and kidnapping South Korean filmmakers. All these tactics will elevate your profile and make people revere you.

Willie & Boyd's Notes:

Richter and Lachey present some frightening scenarios in this chapter. Scenarios that have prompted us to review the way we're treating our sensitive personal information. Poorly guarded passwords and e-mail accounts are sitting ducks for hackers. Throwing credit card offers and other private documents into the recycling bin without shredding them leaves them exposed for theft. But a continued reliance on paper shredders may contribute to an apocalyptic takeover by the very machines we've blindly entrusted to keep us safe.

We're still looking into this machine takeover theory. Maybe the machines really are lulling us into a false sense of security before staging a massive revolution. Whenever we ask the Bills for evidence to support this claim, they seem to only answer with stern questions, like "Do you remember the movie *Short Circuit?* How about *Short Circuit 2?!!* Do you want to live in that world?! Do you?!" or "Which sounds better: controlling your own destiny, or answering to every whim of your goddamned toaster oven??? Hello??!" The logic seems a little loose, but their intensity sells the message. We need to be careful who, and what, we trust. Especially our office machines. Staples supply store is a virtual training ground for the armies that will rise up against us.

Fortunately, Richter and Lachey also give us some affordable and easy-to-implement solutions for avoiding all those problems. And we've taken that information to heart. At this very moment, a motorcade is ready in the parking garage, waiting to take us to the Buffalo Sabres vs. Columbus Blue Jackets game tonight. A second motorcade, with Boyd and Willie body doubles (Emilio Estevez and Anthony Michael Hall, respectively), will emerge just before, and lead any surveillance teams of cyber thieves on a wild-goose chase sure to last until the Zamboni leaves the ice.

Thank you, Bills. Step by step, we're building our prosperous new lives on the strong foundation of your wisdom. Lives that are protected by Big Beefy Guys in tight black shirts. We're sorry if we ever seemed to doubt you.

Section 6

Your Future

Chapter Thirteen

Saving for College

In the journey of life, there are a handful of major events that shape one's destiny. Getting laid for the first time. Getting married. Having a child. Getting freaked out and bailing on that situation. Moving into a houseboat. Leasing a Kawasaki motorcycle. Getting married a second time (to a younger, hotter chick with no needy kids). Having another child (son of a bitch, how does this keep happening?!). Well, sending this second, unintended, unwanted child to college is another of these epic events.

Ever hear of the old saying, "You can't see the trees in a

forest?" Well, the process of saving for college tuition is a lot like that forest. It's dark, foreboding, and tough to see through. It's like the Yoda island in *Empire Strikes Back*, except you don't have a sweet light saber or Jedi powers to cover room and board. The following e-mail was sent to us from a loyal fan of our frequently-cited-by-world-leaders,* Internet-only investment show, **DOLLAR BILLS**. As you'll see, Dean Sunderson needs some serious help figuring out how to navigate his way out of the dark forest and prepare his family for his daughter's impending college education. He needs to see the goddamned trees.

From: Dean Sunderson
To: The Dollar Bills
Cc:
Subject: Help! College tuition payments!

Dear Dollar Bills,
I'm a longtime fan of your show, and hoping you can help me out with a problem. My wife and I have had to do quite a bit of belt tightening with the economy the way it is these days, but our daughter is two years away from college, and we really need to keep saving. I make $65,000 a year and

---

*The show was once sued by Michael Dukakis, after we prank-called him and repeatedly said his last name for like five minutes straight. We didn't realize his staff could track our phone number through caller ID. But take a joke, man! You'd think he'd appreciate the free press.

we have about $28,000 saved right now. My wife is working at the library three days a week to help out with the day-to-day expenses, but I'm worried we won't be ready when those tuition bills start rolling in. I'm really lost, and feel like I'm in a serious financial emergency! What should I do?

Sincerely,
Dean Sunderson
Shaker Heights, OH

Clearly, Dean is a guy who will need a lot of help to get where he needs to be. Some people pick it up quickly. Others (Dean) need some extra coddling. Primarily, what Dean fails to understand is the fact that achieving success comes down to making the big picture, not just the little details, work in your favor. He could save every last dime he touches, and still not reach his goal, because he's not able to see the bigger forces at work.

What Dean can't seem to grasp here is that it's more than setting up a weekly direct deposit into a college fund. It's about letting the college come to *you*. You make that happen, and you've already won. Below is the response we sent to Dean, showing him how to make that happen.

From: The Dollar Bills
To: Dean Sunderson
Cc:
Subject: RE: Help! College tuition payments!

Okay, Dean. First things first, your wife should quit her job. Right now. Stop reading this for a moment, and yell to her that she's not going to work today. Dean, lesson 1: If you want to BE successful, you have to LOOK successful. The wives of successful businessmen don't work. Period. Sign her up for tennis lessons and have her donate half your savings to an environmental nonprofit group. **"Philanthropist"** is code for "super-rich." Also, donating to "green" groups usually leads to your family becoming a "green" group. "Green," as in the kind of green that's money. Not the other kind that's grass and environment things.

Plain English Guide to Confusing Financial Terms
Philanthropist: Code for "super-rich." Also may have something to do with the study of dinosaurs and cavemen, which, coincidentally, is usually done by rich scientists.

Next thing you should do, Dean, is go out and buy three suits. One navy blue, one gray, and one dark with pinstripes. Three buttons, or double-breasted. Tapered at the waist. Full break on the pants. And get pocket squares for each. You should also invest in a premium blazer and yachting pants, for summer months and casual business meetings at the pier.

Why all the haberdashery, you ask? Because the university admissions boards will take note of your new, top-of-the-line menswear. The brass will be all the more interested in accepting your daughter because of the big-time donations they assume a man of your means willl float them for a new freshman cafeteria, or at least some new vending machines outside the rec center. Don't get all freaked out, Dean—you don't actually have to ever give them money. Just let them *believe* you will.

Hey, who's the rich guy in the well-tailored suit? I'd sure love to have his daughter come to my college because of the large donations he'd probably give us.

If you really want to get down to the brass tacks of it all, we think college is a waste of time. Especially for a girl. Dean, let me get this straight: You're going to spend all your money so your daughter can get a degree to marry someone? Be smart. But if you've got your heart set on it, keep reading.

And Jesus, Dean. "I'm in a serious financial emergency"?? Are you *serious* with that bitch-ass whining? Don't ever, ever admit that. You know what we do every time we go bankrupt? We sure as hell don't panic and use the word "emergency." But we *do* rent a Buick LeSabre for the day and drive around with the top down, holding three-olive martinis. Again, if you don't LOOK successful, you're not, plain and simple.

Remember, as this graph illustrates, wealth is 20 percent liquidity and 68 percent perception. The other 18 percent is made up of fine Scandinavian cologne and velvet slippers.

The Breakdown of Wealth

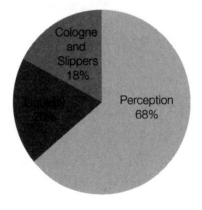

Dean, the best thing you can do for your daughter right now is to show her what success looks like. Here's a hint: It wears Hugo Boss suits, exotic cologne, and drives a pre-owned American sports car. Trust us, the universities will take notice, and come knocking.

We also suggest you try these numbers on the Pick 6 tonight: 51, 21, 2, 24, 18, 27. Those are the numbers of Yankee greats: Bernie Williams, Paul O'Neill, Derek Jeter, Tino Martinez, Scott Brosius, and Butch Wynegar. Try them every night until they hit. You're welcome. Let us know how it works out, Dean.

Millionairely Yours,
Bill Richter and Bill Lachey
The Dollar Bills

As you can see, a few simple moves, and Dean can transform himself from a frightened, whiny bitch, to a high profile, in-demand, proud father of a college valedictorian. If you happen to find yourself in a position like Dean's, you need to listen closely: It's time for you to man-up and spend your savings the right way: LeSabre, tailored suits, tennis lessons, and a few well-timed philanthropistic maneuvers. Trust us, your kid will learn more by watching you run shit than he or she ever will in six years of college. Good luck.

DOLLAR BILLS TIP #111

Did you know that the IRS is really a government hoax? Just like Area 51, Studio 54, Y2K, or Bigfoot—it doesn't actually exist. The pundits would have you believe you need to pay taxes every year, but all you're really doing is lining the pockets of fatcat Washington bureaucrats. We haven't paid taxes since the Bush administration (the older one).

Willie & Boyd's Notes:

Richter and Lachey outline some pretty unconventional methods in this chapter. We were both fortunate enough to attend a great university, and our parents worked extremely hard to be able to provide us with this opportunity. So far as we can tell, this process did not involve tennis, LeSabres, or martinis, so it has taken some time to work through this information.

From our experience, "let the college come to you" works if you're a prodigious athlete or student. That's a good strategy for LeBron James, but not as much for our young kids. It seems like a long shot that schools will throw out scholarships based solely on how sweet someone's suit is. But Richter and Lachey stress that it is precisely this narrow-mindedness that keeps most people from achieving their dreams. The guys haven't led us astray yet, so we went out to Syms menswear and got ourselves a closetful of suits and double-breasted blazer/slacks combos. Charcoal gray is the color we have laid out for our daughters' future college visits. The Bills stress that we need to go even beyond what's in their notes, so we stocked up on musk and velvet Ferragamo slippers as well. Look out, admissions boards: Here we come (in fifteen years when our kids are grown up)!

Chapter Fourteen

Planning for Retirement

Social Security. Medicare. 401(k). What do these have in common? They're three things you will *not* need for retirement. Do you really want to be known around your super-exclusive, openly discriminatory golf club as the guy who relies on the government to take care of him when he decides to hang up his suspenders and Bluetooth? Do you want to perpetually nurse the man-boob of Uncle Sam, waiting like a puppy dog for the mailman to deliver your Social Security check? That's just embarrassing. If you follow the simple instructions we have laid out in this book, you'll spend your retirement

People Who Use Social Security

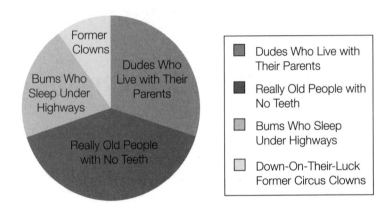

full-body-massaging the boobs of Cleveland Browns cheer-leaders as you cruise Lake Huron on your sick Boston Whaler with a cooler full of MGD and not a care in the world.

Here's the big mistake most people make, and if we've seen it once we've seen it a million times: They get so wrapped up in "planning for retirement" all their working lives that they forget the best retirement plan is to just get rich as shit, plain and simple. Every moment you spend "saving" is another moment you're not earning. The Dollar Bills commissioned an extensive study that revealed the following: People who save regularly are 94 percent less rich than people who are just flat-out rich. The numbers don't lie.

People Who Are the Richest Study Results v.1

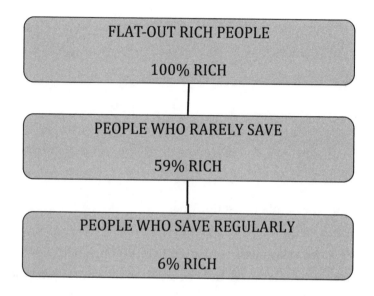

FLAT-OUT RICH PEOPLE

100% RICH

PEOPLE WHO RARELY SAVE

59% RICH

PEOPLE WHO SAVE REGULARLY

6% RICH

And just so you don't think we are doctoring the numbers, here's another perspective. Take a look:

People Who Are the Richest
Study Results v.2

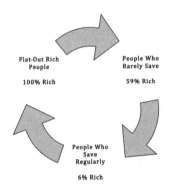

Again, the numbers just don't lie.

Rather than waste your time here talking about how to put your pennies away over decades while working for the man, we'll refer you back to the previous chapters of this manifesto. Just get rich. No pennies. No working for the man. Just mountains of sweet, green cash and pure, uncut Colombian cocaine. How's that for a retirement plan?

A couple of important notes about these demeaning government welfare programs that the feds try to suck you into. First, Social Security doesn't kick in until you're like 75 years old. (No one knows the exact age on this because the so-called "government" refuses to release the information. Just like the JFK assassination.) In case you haven't figured it out by now, there's one little problem with this: Your goal is to retire by the age of 40. What good is that dirty welfare money going to do you when you're knocking on death's door 35 years later? None. Forget about it. When the Social Security checks start to come, use them to roll the massive joints you'll be smoking to "ease your arthritis" on the beach outside your all-inclusive resort* in Negril.

Second, always refer to Medicare as "Medi-See-If-I-Care." Totally awesome put-down that shows you're swimming in greenbacks and you don't need the government's money: "Thanks for the handout offer, but I'll be paying for this quadruple bypass surgery in cash. What do I owe you? Ten grand? Here's twenty grand. Keep the change." You could say something like that if you get a live person on the phone, but usually payment is rendered on an automated system or even just done on the Medicare Web site.

Now, when you do retire a wealthy young man or broad (it's unlikely, obviously, that broads would be able to retire at 40 since they're not tough or aggressive, but we have to put that in here to comply with bullshit **Title IX Laws**), you're going to want to go out with great fanfare. Michael Jordan and Brett Favre are your models here. Create "Will he or won't he?" mystery around your retirement by leaking anonymous

---

*Read the fine print on the Jamaican all-inclusives. Sometimes top-shelf liquor and cliff-diving are extra.

stories to various industry blogs and internal newsletters that suggest you're thinking of stepping aside. Keep them guessing until finally you hold a dramatic retirement press conference with your hot, crying girlfriend at your side (e.g., Kobe's famous retirement presser).

Plain English Guide to Confusing Financial Terms
Title IX Laws: Laws that force men to treat women like men, but still like women too. In other words, you have to act like a woman is your business equal, but can't ask her if she was the one who ripped ass in the break room, or mention anything about your balls. Total double standard.

The business world will be rocked to its core by your abrupt departure. You'll be remembered at expensive retirement dinners as one of the greats, you'll be showered with gold watches and hilarious toasts, and more importantly, you'll get to cash out your stock options. Anyone want to go for a **golden parachute** ride?!

Plain English Guide to Confusing Financial Terms
Golden Parachute: The corporate equivalent of a golden shower. Tradition dictates that when an elite executive retires, he jumps off the roof of the office building, pops the parachute, and starts pissing down onto the parking lot and smoking patio below. Typically nets lots of laughs, then everyone heads to the going-away party at Benihana.

Then, when your company goes into the crapper for a couple years while you're gone, you un-retire and ride back in on a white horse to save the day (you literally should ride bareback on a white stallion into the office on that first day back—make sure you pack some low-fat trail mix for the long ride, some ointment for those inevitable saddle sores, and some carrots for the horse). Retire again a year later, then rinse, repeat, and watch your legend grow.

The multiple comeback worked for Jordan and it worked for Favre—have you checked their net worth lately? Well into the low billions. You can look that shit up if you don't believe us. With your highly publicized comeback to the business world, you can be certain that you'll have Hanes and Wrangler knockin' on your door too, ready to talk long-term, multimillion-dollar endorsement deals. I'm just guessing here, but I'm pretty sure Michael Jordan and Brett Favre aren't living on Social Security and Medicare—unless *Social Security* and *Medicare* are the names of their respective yachts docked in Grand Cayman. They might be living on those part-time.

Bottom line: Retirement planning is for working stiffs. Let those people save their money for shuffleboard and early-bird specials in Boca. Follow the Dollar Bills' guide to instant wealth and your retirement will consist of jumbo shrimp cocktails and yacht racing in the Caribbean with Jordan and Favre (and probably Jaromir Jagr once he hangs up the skates).

Remember why you're doing all of this

Take time to appreciate the finer things in life, like champagne in plastic cups (which you can chuck off the roof after you pound the booze!).

Willie & Boyd's Notes:

We feel like we're well on our way to retirement thanks to Richter and Lachey's methods, but we're not there yet so we can't draw any conclusions about their advice. We assume it's spot-on. Anything that involves smokin' hot cheerleaders from Cleveland can't be wrong, right?

Boyd did send out a preliminary press release to drum up some interest about the kind of dramatic, Jordanesque retirement press conference the Bills suggested. So far we have a firm commitment only from a guy who writes a "black-market organ dealing" blog in Fort Wayne, Indiana. Neither of us can remember sending him the release—he just said he'd love to come see us and maybe stay for a long weekend. We shall see!

Loaded!

The Plain English Guide to Confusing Financial Terms

Perhaps the most critical factor in your achieving life-changing success is being able to "talk the talk." Not sure what that means? Then you'll want to pay special attention to our "Plain English Guide to Confusing Financial Terms." This comprehensive guide provides simple, Everyman definitions to complicated industry words. This knowledge will enable you to work these key terms into your daily jargon immediately, and start reaping the rewards.

Amortization: A love of money. From "amore," the Italian word for love.

Ancillary Revenue: Extra cash derived from an already brilliant idea. Like when you open a lucrative ice cream parlor and then sell drugs and bootleg movies out the back door for a little added cheese.

Annuity: Something that happens every year (e.g., the Miss Universe pageant, a presidential election, and Dick Clark's *Rockin' New Year's Eve*).

Appraisal: To shower with praise after a successful real estate deal.

APR: Primary competition to NPR. Similar to AFC/NFC in football, or AL/NL in baseball. Same competitive spirit holds true for radio.

Arbitrage: A line of French bath and body products.

ARM: Duh! Look down, dumbass!

Ask for the Order: Used frequently in high-stakes negotiations. Typically has one of two meanings: 1) Make your demands and close the deal, or, in some cases, 2) Order the surf-and-turf, or another pricey entrée, if the negotiations are taking place over lunch and said lunch is being paid for by your opponent.

Balance Sheet: A ledger where one keeps track of one's balance and plyometric exercises (number of reps, number of sets).

Balloon Note: The deed to a luxury zeppelin. Another oft missed investment gold mine if the price is right.

Bill of Sale: One of England's most famous aristocrats, a cousin and drinking buddy to William of York.

Blue Chip Stocks: Named for the stock of liberal, bleeding-heart companies. Derived from the blue tortilla chips trend in the mid- to late aughts, started by organic, vegetarian, animal rights activists. Blue tortilla chips? Gimme a break. Buy/sell these stocks with caution. You never know what kind of left-wing sanctions the company may impose on you.

Bridge Loan: Leveraging assets (in this case, magic beads) to generate a loan with which to build a bridge. Also applies to toll plazas, piers, and large docks.

Buydown: A chain of dollar stores found throughout Arizona and New Mexico.

Call Option: If someone gives you a Call Option, it means you've got the option to give them a ring anytime you want—to grab lunch, play squash, or see if they want to go ferret hunting over the weekend. This can prove to be extremely valuable with the right contact.

Closing Costs: The process of closing a retail store. Cashing out the register, sweeping up, and pulling down the security shutters after locking up.

Commodity: Stuff that everybody wants, traded openly on an exchange. Copper, pork bellies, and Mark McGwire rookie cards are all examples.

Cottage Industry: Booming in the Swiss Alps these days.

Credit Default Swap (CDS): Definition unknown, but all that swappin' sounds kind of kinky.

Current Ratio: The ratio of currency to the current market rates.

Cyber: Awesome word that makes anything sound cutting-edge, like "I'm chillin' at a cyber-café," or "check out these new cyber-pants," or "I'm gonna catch a quick cyber-nap." Also a kickass martial arts film starring Jean-Claude Van Damme (the Muscles from Brussels).

Depreciation: When the value of something goes down, like the home you bought for no money down at $500,000 in 2006 that's worth $100,000 today. Oops!

Derivative: When an artist rips off ideas or material from another artist. Example: Vanilla Ice stealing the hook for "Ice Ice Baby" from Queen's "Under Pressure." Same principle holds true for investing. Some people innovate, others derivatate.

Diversification: Getting certified as a deep-sea diver. Deep-sea dives (spearing endangered starfish) and days spent on luxury yachts are important leisure activities for big-time hitters.

Dividend: Something that pays off down the road. Like an investment in flying cars.

Dollar Cost Averaging: How much your dollar costs. Typically $1.00 unless there is a service charge.

Economy of Scale: Refers to the local economy in Scale, a city in southern Italy.

Elevator Pitch: Practicing your pitching delivery for your co-ed, slow-pitch softball league while riding the elevator up to an important meeting, or down a floor to use a different crapper.

Escrow: Awesome Christian rock band out of Tulsa.

Fair Market Value: The value of something you buy at the county fair. Always add 15 percent when you position this item for resale in the big city.

Fannie Mae: Maker of fine baked goods. Company named after founder's grandma Fannie Mae. Famous for breakfast cakes based on Fannie's hundred-year-old recipe.

Firewall: In the early days of the Internet, companies like Apple and Microsoft literally built huge walls around their offices and set them on fire, so that spies and intruders would be kept at bay. This technique, while effective, did not translate to the general consumer. Now, firewalls are installed, on a much smaller scale, within the actual computer. This is precisely why your laptop gets hot if you use it for a long time.

Fixed Asset: An asset (i.e., a thing) that has been repaired, and thus, has increased in value.

Floating Asset with High Liquidity: Something you own that floats.

Foreclosure: When some guys from the bank come to help you move out of your old place into a sweet new loft with exposed brick walls.

Found Money: Money that you find on the Street or in a hidden spot; the best kind of money there is. Not to be confused with "Stolen Money." That's the stuff you score when you siphon cash from your niece's Girl Scout cookie sales.

401(k) Plan: Phone plan that covers the area code (401) for all of Rhode Island.

Freddie Mac: Hard-hitting, two-time Pro Bowl safety for the Tampa Bay Buccaneers in the mid-'80s. Died at the peak of his career in a tragic roller-coaster accident at Busch Gardens.

GDP: Great Deal, Partner!

GNP: Got a Narc Present (someone who works for the government).

Golden Parachute: The corporate equivalent of a golden shower. Tradition dictates that when an elite executive retires, he jumps off the roof of the office building, pops the parachute, and starts pissing down onto the parking lot and smoking patio below. Typically nets lots of laughs, then everyone heads to the going-away party at Benihana.

Hedge Fund: A fund that oversees other funds "from the hedges." In other words, a "big brother," of sorts, for investment funds.

Ice You: Slang for "Isolate you," i.e., lock you in a musty, cramped room until you submit to certain demands, like a performance-based bonus, or a limit on your cell minutes.

Investment Bank: A bank where all the tellers wear vests.

IPO: Investment Plan Overload. In a fast-moving market, novice investors often plan too much, and miss the boat. These people need handholding and shepherding.

Jumbo Loan: Shorthand for "Jumbo Shrimp Loan." Loans used frequently in fishing villages but with relevance all the way up the ladder, to Wall Street. After all, jumbo shrimp are a valuable, tradable commodity.

LIBOR: Lateral Investment Buyouts and Outsourced Revenue. Don't worry about what it "means"—technically it has never been defined—just remember to keep your LIBOR scores up.)

LLC: Important initials to put after your start-up company's name for credibility. Nobody knows for certain the real meaning. It's like putting Ph.D. or M.D. at the end of your own name. A meaningless addendum that'll make your business card really pop.

Margin: A low-fat substitute for butter. Tastes a little bit different, but totally worth it.

Market Capitalization: Capitalizing on the fresh produce at an open-air organic market.

Maturity: Finally taking the Guns 'n' Roses, Dan Marino, and Kathy Ireland posters off the wall. Guess we'll never be mature because those posters ain't coming down!

Mom-and-Pop Company: A company (Lachey Laser Tag is one of the most celebrated examples) that services lots of hot moms, and thus becomes a business with tons of pop, i.e., flashiness and/or Diet Fanta.

Monopoly: Only the best board game ever invented. Sorry, Chutes and Ladders (hint: invest in Atlantic Avenue and thank us later)!

Mutual Fund: A fund that is mutually approved by at least four or five Hedge Fund managers.

No-Cost Loan: A loan that doesn't cost you anything. At all. The best kind.

Operating Income: Income you set aside in the event you need major surgery, like a gall bladder transplant, or a new set of cans for your wife/girlfriend.

Passive Income: Income that gets "passed along" to you from a charity.

P/E Ratio: The Penis-Envy ratio of your business adversaries. A monster hose is still your best competitive advantage.

Penny Stock: The amount of raw, molten bronze a company that makes pennies has on hand at any given moment.

Philanthropist: Code for "super-rich." Also may have something to do with the study of dinosaurs and cavemen, which, coincidentally, is usually done by rich scientists.

Portfolio: The folder, often made of rich leather and not unlike a Trapper Keeper, that holds the printouts of one's investments. Allows for easy movement of investments between office, home, and sauna.

Power of Attorney: Same concept as "Power of Doctor," but in the legal sense. Basically, doctors and lawyers are typically rich and powerful.

Predatory Loan: Loans made to predators (e.g., cheetahs, crocodiles, jacked dudes with brass knuckles, and, most importantly, savvy entrepreneurs).

Preferred Stock: The kind that makes you rich as balls. Would you "prefer" some other kind?

Prime Rate: Killer steakhouse in Hilton Head, SC. Don't miss the garlic fries!

Prospectus: Professional gold digger. Also the old guy in *Gladiator*.

Revolving Debt: Debt created and carried by companies that specialize in manufacturing revolving doors, like the ones you would see at a 5-star hotel. Typically these doors are made from mercury, which makes them light enough to spin smoothly. Mercury, however, is extremely pricey. Hence, the high debt ratio for these companies.

Right of First Refusal: A power move in negotiation where you tell everyone to fuck off. Always emphasized with a phone slammed down (landline) or thrown at your assistant (cellular).

Royalty Trust: The respect and faithfulness to people of royal descent. And for good reason. Just try and name three people more trusted than the King of England. That's what we thought. Get on his good side.

SEC: Hands down, the toughest conference in college football.

Seed Stock: Literally, stock in a seed and livestock company. Nonliterally, building a large supply of your man-seed which you can later sell for a hefty sum. Note: requires a special centrifuge device and an extra ice-box in your garage.

Short Sale: Every spring at Banana Republic, Palm Desert Outlets location. Cargo, cotton chino, and summer linen all 40 percent off. The best!

Socioeconomics: The study of poor people being bitter at successful, rich, charismatic people. Also the name of an underground Dutch techno group.

Structured Investment Vehicle (SIV): The vehicles used by Wall Street traders to travel from home to stock exchange and back again. Most are sweet Mercedes or Bentleys with curtains in the back.

Subprime Mortgage: Money lent for investments in nuclear submarines and other prime underwater submersibles.

Sweat Equity: Your investment of perspiration and hard work in a business project, in a game of shirts-and-skins hoops, or just in power humping some broad you met at the gym.

Title IX Laws: Laws that force men to treat women like men, but still like women too. In other words, you have to act like a woman is your business equal, but can't ask her if she was the one who ripped ass in the break room, or mention anything about your balls. Total double standard.

Too Big to Fail: When a Wall Street company is so awesome that it literally can't fail. Also the title of an upcoming Rocco Siffredi adult film.

Underwriting: The opposite of "Overwriting," something we counsel our clients to avoid. Quite simply, the less you put down on paper, the better. We always favor a handshake deal and verbal confirmation of deal points/meeting places/abort codes over something in writing which can be later used against you.

Working Capital: Also known as Headquarters. Where the big work decisions are made.

Yield: You don't have to come to a full stop, but slow down and check for traffic before proceeding.

CONGRATULATIONS!

You are now ready to get LOADED!

In Conclusion

By Willie and Boyd

That "Plain English Guide to Confusing Financial Terms" makes for a perfect bow on this neatly wrapped Dollar Bills package of financial wisdom. And make no mistake, their wisdom is a gift to all of us. Punctuating the theme of the *Loaded!* manifesto, the glossary pulls back the curtain on a system where smoke, mirrors, squirting flowers, trick birthday candles, disappearing ink, loaded dice, games of three-card monte, sawed-in-half magician's assistants, "there's a quarter behind your ear" tricks, and general gobbledygook are used to hide simple truths from good, hardworking people like you. Bill

Richter and Bill Lachey cut through the fog to reveal the secrets that the financial magicians don't want you to know.

A "balloon note" sure sounds complicated, but thanks to the Bills' "Plain English Guide" we know it's nothing more than the deed to a luxury zeppelin. Sure, we've heard the term "P/E ratio" before, but we always thought it was some complex economic principle we'd never understand. Now we know it's just shorthand for talking about the size of your wiener in a business setting. And that big, scary word "escrow"? It's only scary if you're not a fan of awesome Tulsa-based Christian rock bands.

Look, we can't vouch for all the claims made in the pages you've just read—some of that shit just can't be true. But what we *can* vouch for are results. Our families cried bloody murder when we started buying pontoon party boats, putting exotic sharks in our pools, bidding on rare Picassos, building exclusive golf clubs in Afghanistan, and entering into possibly gay relationships with our rich uncles. Our closest friends thought we'd been had by Internet con artists. Can you blame them? We're the first to admit that it all sounds pretty nuts. And, sure, when the money started to dry up without much hope for a return on our highly leveraged, bank-breaking investments and our marriages began to dissolve before our eyes, we thought about abandoning the Dollar Bills ship. We can admit that now. But Richter and Lachey implored us to blindly place our trust in their unproven methods, even threatening at one point to burn down our homes with Molotov cocktails if we dropped out. That's how strongly they believe in their system.

One rainy night, as the two of us sat slumped on Lachey's leather sectional couch eating his famous queso dip and wondering where exactly this Dollar Bills program was leading us, we happened to flip to the movie *Karate Kid* on Starz. And it was there, at our lowest point, that a teenaged martial arts apprentice restored our hope. We watched a young man played by Ralph Macchio go through weeks of painting fences, sanding floors, and waxing cars for some weird little Japanese dude. Macchio was frustrated because he had come to Pat Morita's house to learn karate, not to perform slave labor. When Macchio finally had had enough, he started to storm out of Morita's crib and forever swear off his dream of becoming a black belt. But Morita stopped Macchio just in time to show him the light.

Morita revealed that the motions Macchio had been practicing over and over again for all those exhausting weeks— "Paint the fence!" "Wax on, wax off!"—actually were sick karate moves. Macchio *was* a black belt and he didn't even know it. All that painting, sanding, and waxing had done more than save Morita an assload of money on contractors. It had empowered Macchio to take down his hated Cobra Kai rivals at the All Valley Karate Championship, even though he checked in at an almost sickly 135 pounds. His prize? A young Elisabeth Shue. Not bad.

As the final credits rolled, we looked at each other through eyes welled with tears, understanding that we were in a mutual state of epiphany—we call it our *Karate Kid* moment. At the exact moment we watched Macchio execute a perfect crane kick to finish off Billy Zabka in the championship match, the wisdom of the Dollar Bills had come rushing over us. Thanks to Macchio and Morita, we saw clearly that the wealth and prestige exercises we were being put through, from wearing a Bluetooth device 24 hours a day to chain-smoking and smacking the butts of our female colleagues around the office to making our wives quit their jobs, were all part of our training. Turns out we'd been doing our own version of sanding and waxing. We emerged suddenly from the dense trees to see the forest around us. Yes, we were black belts in finance and we didn't even know it. From there, we never looked back. Now we're well on our way to the All Valley "Gettin' Filthy Rich" Championship where we plan to win the trophy and get an Elisabeth Shue of our own (preferably the more hookerish *Leaving Las Vegas* version).

Do we have hard numbers to show the success of the Dollar Bills program? Not yet. But now that you've read *Loaded!* you understand that's not the point. Confusing charts littered with numbers, data, and jargon only cloud a greater, more beautiful picture of personal wealth that is about so much more than money alone. All we can tell you is that every time we roll up to the marina in Delray Beach in our no-money-down leased cigarette boat with a topless mermaid painted on the side, throw the keys to the dockhand, tell him to "keep it close," and fire a wadded-up five-spot in his face, we sure as hell look—and *feel*—rich. And that, the Dollar Bills have taught us, is all that matters.

Author Notes

NBCU Photo Bank

Christopher Ward

Willie Geist is the host of MSNBC's *Way Too Early with Willie Geist* and the co-host of *Morning Joe*. He is the author of the *New York Times* bestseller *American Freak Show*. Geist, who lives in New York with his wife and two children, has been compared to a young Josh Groban.

Boyd McDonnell is a television development and production executive in Los Angeles, where he lives with his wife and three children. This is his first romance novel.

Acknowledgments

To our wives, Paige and Christina, for humoring us, even when we're not humorous. Thank you for your love and encouragement. Also, for being cool about that time you walked in on us wrestling. We were just wrestling. In the dark.

To our children, Ryan, Maris, Myles, Lucie, and George. We believe early childhood education is important, but if it's really your dream to drop out and form a traveling pre-school band, we will support you.

To our siblings, Carter, Clayton, and Libby, our partners in crime for more than thirty years. We mean that quite literally. We all committed a heinous crime together thirty years ago for which we have never been prosecuted.

To our parents: don't beat yourselves up. None of this is your fault.

To Aaron Thacker, Thomas McIntyre, Sweet Louis Burgdorf, Jim and Nicole Cannella, and the mysterious Wealthy Swedish Financier for your willingness to get weird and give this book life.

To the key people who believed in this idea and helped turn it into a book (and an upcoming major motion picture from Tyler Perry): Peter McGuigan at Foundry Literary + Media, Kara Welker at Generate, and Phil Revzin, Laura Chasen, John Karle, Matthew Shear, and Sally Richardson at St. Martin's Press.